PRO TACTICS™

MUSKIE

PRO TACTICS™

MUSKIE

Use the Secrets of the Pros to
Catch More and Bigger Muskie

Jack Burns and Rob Kimm

THE LYONS PRESS
Guilford, Connecticut
An imprint of The Globe Pequot Press

The Lyons Press is an imprint of The Globe Pequot Press.
Pro Tactics is a trademark of Morris Book Publishing, LLC.

Text design by Peter Holm, Sterling Hill Productions

Illustrations by Michael Gellatly

Library of Congress Cataloging-in-Publication Data is available.

ISBN 978-1-59921-278-4

Printed in the United States of America

10 9 8 7 6 5 4 3 2 1

CONTENTS

ACKNOWLEDGMENTS

We'd like to thank the many people who made this book possible. The staff and writers of *The Next Bite—Esox Angler Magazine* for their insights and ideas, the many friends and fellow anglers who supplied photos, and the folks we fish with, who help us put theory into practice.

We'd like to express special gratitude to our friend and photographer Dave Olson for the many beautiful photos that appear throughout this book. His expertise and dedication to this project were invaluable.

Finally, we'd like to thank our families, who have tolerated our temporary preoccupation with this book, as well as our lifelong preoccupation with muskies: Rob's children, Morgan, Marcy, and Ethan, and our wives, Mary and Sara, who support us unstintingly and keep us humble by inevitably catching the biggest fish.

INTRODUCTION

Ask a dedicated muskie angler why he or she pursues muskies so avidly, and the angler will often have a surprisingly difficult time coming up with an answer. Is it how they fight when hooked? Muskies are strong fighters, sure, but a pike of comparable size will fight far longer, and trout and salmon are much more acrobatic. The challenge? Walleyes and bass require far more technical skill. Practically any species you care to name short of sunfish (and perhaps even they) are more discriminating feeders. Success with smallmouth bass can hinge on selecting just the right hue and shape of soft plastic. Muskies happily gnaw on fluorescent orange hunks of wood. And 3-ounce jigs or 8-ounce gobs of soft plastic are considered "finesse tactics."

Press them long enough, and most muskie anglers will finally give in and admit that it's simply this: There's an indefinable *something* about muskies that can cause anglers to pursue them with a passion that borders on madness. Call it an attitude, an aura—call it whatever you wish. Whatever it is, muskies have it. They are unique among freshwater species. For some anglers, the urge to pursue muskies is simply irresistible.

The purpose of this book is to help you become more successful and successful with more consistency, should you follow that irresistible urge. Whether you're a veteran muskie angler with years of experience or a beginner approaching the sport of muskie fishing for the first time, there's something in this book for you. We'll cover the basic biology of muskies and how they differ from their more abundant cousin, the northern pike.

We'll discuss the fundamentals of selecting equipment and tackle. All these things are important. Mostly, though, what you'll find in this book are examples of on-the-water tactics and strategies covering a range of seasons, conditions, situations, and fishing styles. More important, you'll find the thinking behind why different approaches and tactics are applied in the scenarios described.

What you *won't* find a lot of is specific information on lakes or "spots." Though we'll refer to specific bodies of water as examples, you won't find marked maps or "fish here with this lure" handholding.

Why not? Because in the long run, it won't do you much good. In fact, marked maps and oversimplified declarations about how to fish this lake or that spot will hurt your success more than help it. Fish behavior, attitude, forage, water and weather conditions—all change from season to season, day to day. What works today may be a bust tomorrow. You're far better off developing an understanding of the *why* behind developing a particular strategy for catching muskies, given the conditions at hand, than simply being told what to do and how. We can't possibly cover every lake you may fish, or situation you might encounter, but with the information you'll find here, you can better adapt to different waters throughout the season.

CHAPTER ONE

Fish of Legend, Fish of Myth

No fish in fresh water is surrounded by as much myth and mystery as the muskellunge. Muskies have been characterized as wily, voracious, even menacing creatures lurking in the depths, with mysterious and unfathomable habits—so difficult to catch that they have become known as "The Fish of 10,000 Casts." And they're large, of course. Throughout the muskie's range, local legends abound about the tackle-wrecking, nigh-uncatchable monsters that dwell in nearby muskie waters: "Old Mossy," a fish so ancient moss trails from its back; or "Jingle Bells," a fish that has broken off so many anglers' lures she sounds like sleigh bells when she swims.

The stories are charming and entertaining, to be sure. They're very much a part of the history and lore of the sport of muskie fishing. But like most fish stories, they have little basis in truth. In fact, the myths surrounding muskies can often be a hindrance to aspiring muskie anglers because, viewed in that light, muskies can be excused as utterly mysterious, their behavior random, the creature itself unfathomable.

Muskies are fish of myth and legends, but the truth is impressive enough. MARY COLSON-BURNS

The truth is, muskies are just fish. Like any other species, muskies have a life cycle and biology that ultimately determine their behavior throughout the course of the year. Understanding at least the basics of that biology is an important part of a successful and rational approach to catching muskies.

While their cousin the northern pike is truly a worldwide fish, found in Asia, Europe, and North America, the muskie's natural range is a fairly limited slice of North America, centered on the Great Lakes and the upper Mississippi River drainages and extending north into Ontario. Within

Muskies have been introduced in many waters across North America, with impressive results. SARA KIMM

that range, however, muskies inhabit a fairly broad range of waters—from massive Lake Superior to tiny streams in West Virginia. Between those two extremes are a vast array of lakes and rivers large and small; clear, infertile Canadian Shield trout lakes; small, dark-water flowages in northern Wisconsin; mid-mesotrophic lakes in central Minnesota; and rivers like the Mississippi, Wisconsin, and Saint Lawrence. Beyond their natural range, muskies have been introduced in many areas of the country. Today, thanks to those introductions, muskies can be found as far east as the Delaware River; as far west as eastern Colorado; and in southern waters in Missouri, Tennessee, and Kentucky.

Muskies differ from their cousins, the pike, in their habits and biology as well. Pike are highly adaptable, tolerating a wide range of water conditions and thriving in habitats as varied as murky prairie potholes and the brackish Baltic Sea. Large pike are a cool-water creature, preferring water temperatures below the 70-degree Fahrenheit mark, and are found as far north as the Northwest Territories' Kazan River—a near-arctic watershed where summer water temperatures rarely reach 50 degrees. Muskies are far less cosmopolitan. They're less tolerant of turbid or murky waters, very sensitive to the presence of industrial pollutants or agricultural runoff, and tolerate a much narrower range of temperatures. Muskies require waters where summer temperatures frequently reach 70 degrees, limiting their northern range to the English River/Lac Seul system in northwest Ontario.

Pike and muskies, though related, don't always coexist well. Pike spawn immediately after ice-out, far earlier than muskies, and are far more prolific spawners. Muskies are among the last to spawn, when water temperatures reach 48 to 50 degrees. When muskies and pike use similar spawning areas, newly hatched muskie fry are preyed upon by pike fry, which have already begun feeding on fish. In muskie lakes where pike have been introduced, either accidentally or by design, muskies fare poorly.

In lakes or rivers where the two species evolved together, however, muskies and pike coexist just fine, with good populations of both. How is that possible?

The answer lies in the differing strains of muskies. Though there is some debate even among fisheries biologists as to the exact nature of the distinctions, generally speaking, there are at least two different strains of muskies, commonly referred to as the Wisconsin and the Leech Lake or Mississippi strains.

Wisconsin strain muskies spawn in habitat similar to northern pike—flooded vegetation in 15 to 20 inches of water, often in shallow weedy bays or backwaters. Mississippi strain fish spawn offshore in 3 to 6 feet of water over a combination of marl and chara, a type of aquatic vegetation similar to sandgrass. Mississippi strain muskies also spawn twice each season, the second spawn occurring seven to ten days after the first. Biologists suspect that these differences in behavior—spawning well away from typical northern pike spawning and rearing areas, and a second spawn—are adaptations enabling them to compete with their more prolific cousins.

Whether Wisconsin or Mississippi strain, muskies are broadcast spawners, spreading eggs at random throughout spawning areas rather than building nests. A 40-pound female muskie is capable of producing up to 200,000 eggs. Larval muskies feed on insects and zooplankton, changing to a fish diet when they reach 2 inches in size.

Muskies are an apex predator—the very peak of the food chain. As adults, their diet consists almost entirely of other fish. Muskies are opportunistic feeders. If they can catch it and get their mouth around it, it's a potential item on the menu. They eat what's abundant and easy to catch, so their "preferred forage" can vary from one body of water to the next. In one lake the bulk of the muskie population may feed on perch and suckers. In another it may be pelagic, cold-water species like ciscoes and whitefish. Still, they do show general tendencies in what they choose to call dinner.

Research has shown that muskies will select soft-rayed, high-energy species like ciscoes when available, and it is in bodies of water where these forage species are available that muskies grow largest. At certain times of year, understanding the interaction between muskies and particular forage species can be a critical factor in finding and catching muskies.

Like any other top predator, muskies are a low-density species. Even on good muskie waters, muskies are a rarity in terms of their overall population. On many muskie waters in their natural range, a population density of 0.25 fish per acre is considered high.

The low-density nature of muskie populations has significant implications for anglers. Some of those implications are mental, some are purely practical, and some are ethical.

Fishing for muskies requires an adjustment in anglers' expectations—and their definition of success. Consider the results of a typical day on the water. For most muskie anglers, a three-fish day is cause for celebration—high-fives all around at the dock. Catch three bass in a day, and it's a disaster. With few fish overall, the learning curve with muskies can be steep, and many beginning muskie anglers, frustrated with their lack of immediate success, give up altogether.

In practical terms, the nature of muskie populations dictates an efficient approach to catching them. Muskies aren't particularly difficult to catch. What *is* difficult is locating them, identifying their attitude on a given day, and figuring out what presentation might be successful. Even on a good day, on good water, the number of chances an angler may have to contact and catch a muskie is pretty low. Simply put, the greatest hurdle to overcome in being successful with muskies is the math. In order to maximize the frequency of those opportunities, being as efficient as possible is a necessity. What's efficient depends on the fish's location, conditions, forage, and water type. Much of this book will be focused on finding efficient approaches in different situations on the water.

Finally, the relative rarity of muskies places an ethical obligation on muskie anglers as well. Muskies are few in number, and a slow-growing species besides. On many waters, a trophy-class fish—in the 48-inch-plus range—can be twenty years old.

The low density and slow growth of muskies makes catch-and-release a critical aspect of the sport of muskie fishing. There's ample evidence that muskies that have been released can be caught and enjoyed multiple times.

On lakes with native muskie populations, kept fish mean lost genetics and fewer fish available to reproduce and sustain the population. The recent history of muskie fishing includes some dark episodes where relatively untouched muskie waters (Lac Seul and Lake Wabigoon in northwest Ontario, Canada) were overexploited nearly to the point of no return by anglers harvesting personal trophies.

More could be said about the importance of catch-and-release as an angling ethic—enough to fill a book all its own. But the point is this: Let them go. They're too valuable a resource to catch only once.

Muskies are a low-density species, and releasing them is a critical part of the sport.
SARA KIMM

CHAPTER TWO

Muskies–
The Mental Game

Ten percent of the muskie anglers catch 90 percent of the muskies."
Fact or myth? Probably a fact. Provable? Certainly not.

But as extreme as that statement sounds, it may even be an
understatement. For one thing, 10 percent of the people who fish muskies
probably do 90 percent of the muskie fishing. Those are the hard-core
muskie anglers. Because you're reading this book, you're probably in that
"elite" group. (Only when discussing muskie fishing can we interchange
"hard-core" and "elite" with a straight face.)

But let's look at that 10/90 thing a little closer. Even among the hard-
core/elite anglers, there seem to be a few who catch more and bigger
muskies than the rest of us. We honestly think that it's more like this: "Two
percent of the muskie anglers catch 90 percent of the muskies." Seriously.

What is their secret? What are they doing differently? That is what
we're here to discuss. The two authors of this book have a combined fifty-
five years of muskie fishing experience to draw upon. But that's nothing. As
magazine editors, columnists, and writers, we are in constant contact with

many of those pros who catch more and bigger muskies than everyone else. Real "pros." The 2 percent. We work with, and frequently fish with, some of the best guides in the business, some of the best tournament professionals, and people who can catch muskies under the pressure of TV cameras.

When we discuss pro muskie tactics, we are talking about tactics we have learned from professionals.

There are a lot of ways to catch a muskie. The problem with all the stories and theories that you hear and read about is that most of them are true. They were true on occasion. A particular presentation worked often enough. The theory behind it sounds reasonable. And who can argue with an "expert" holding up a 54-inch muskie?

That's the thing about muskie fishing. So few muskies are caught by any one angler that no one can really prove anything. There is little statistically reliable data. A panfish or walleye expert is able to refine tactics

There are many ways to catch fish like this. All of them work—at least sometimes.
LUKE RONNESTRAND

and presentation techniques by catching thousands of fish. A muskie angler? One per day? One per week? These fish produce stories, not statistics. The trick to consistent success is to move past the stories and myths and theories, and to develop a way to think about muskie fishing like a pro.

Let's look at some of the factors that the pros take into account before they apply their tactics and techniques. Call it the "tactical dilemma." What factors should we look at before we build a strategy?

Seasonal Factors

Through the seasons, a muskie's behavior is influenced by its basic needs. Muskies need to eat, breathe, and reproduce. Muskies also need to avoid predators. Seasonal factors and seasonal priorities affect muskie location and mood and even help determine the presentations that work best. In other words, any discussion of tactics has to start with the seasonal muskie fishing scenarios.

A note about seasons: The muskie's range extends from a few hundred miles into Ontario and Quebec, down to Arkansas, Tennessee, and North Carolina. Late June in northwest Ontario often means that the muskie's spawning time is coming to a close and the fishing season is just getting started. Late June in the southern United States means that a great fishing window is closing, because water temperatures will soon be too high to fish safely. To allow for seasonal variation across this wide muskie range, we usually define seasons according to water temperatures and environmental changes instead of by specific dates. In describing our muskie fishing seasons, we will focus on the northern tier of U.S. lakes, rivers, and flowages and on Canadian Shield waters.

Postspawn to Early Summer
(May into late June in the northern tier)
This period is often the time of the muskie season opener. In many states and provinces, the season is closed in spring to protect spawners. (But even where the regulations do not protect spawning muskies, we hope you do so voluntarily.) The theme of this period is the muskie's transition from spawn recovery into aggressive feeding. The good news for us is that muskies are hungry and "stupid" (uneducated) after a winter of little eating and little

or no fishing pressure. This is also a time of developing weed growth and rising water temperatures.

Summer Peak
(July in the northern tier)

This is one of the two best times to be muskie fishing. It is a time of peak feeding, peak weed growth, and rising water temperatures. But it is also a time of peak fishing pressure, peak tourism, and peak boat traffic. The key here is that you must consider both the muskie's nature and the affect of other anglers.

Mid- to Late Summer
(August in the northern tier)

Also known as dog days, this is a period defined by stability. Muskies are in their established summer routines and locations. It is a time of high water temperatures and still-high fishing pressure. Muskies are in classic predictable locations, and they are still getting pounded.

Early Fall
(Usually September in the northern tier)

This period begins with a sustained decline in water temperatures. It is a time of transition, as summer patterns fall apart and muskies start to move to fall locations. There are also some gradual environmental changes happening. Weeds are beginning to die off as water temperatures drop through the 60s and down toward turnover (usually the mid-50s). Muskies can be at all depths, from extreme shallows to deep hard-bottomed spots.

Mid- to Late Fall
(October into early November in the northern tier)

This period extends from turnover to ice-up (where applicable). Mid- to late fall is prime time for big muskies. Weeds die, so shallow weed-oriented baitfish move out to the main breakline. Open-water (pelagic) baitfish move into the main breakline to stage for spawning. This concentration of baitfish attracts hungry muskies to the breaklines, to the deep edges of classic structure. On some reservoir/river systems, there is a migration of fish populations toward wintering areas. Muskies often set up in ambush on these migration routes, or even cruise them in a more active hunt.

Environmental Factors

Environmental factors start with the type of water the muskies live in. Freshwater lakes can be classified by their geological age: eutrophic, mesotrophic, or oligotrophic.

Some of the most important factors that derive from water type include the muskie population density, the water's "trophy" potential, available forage, water clarity or stain, algae blooms, fluctuating water levels, presence or lack of weeds, rock structure, and other structure, even the amount of fishing pressure the muskies are exposed to.

Eutrophic lakes are geologically old. They are shallow, fertile, warm, and weedy; often have darker water; and are not particularly known for producing trophy muskies. A healthy eutrophic lake will often have panfish, largemouth bass, and sometimes a few muskies. A sick one will feature carp and bullheads.

Oligotrophic lakes are geologically young. They are deep, cold, clear, and relatively sterile, with few weeds and a lot of rocks. Oligotrophic lakes often include lake trout and big northern pike. Muskies, when present, will be low in number, but those muskies can be huge.

Mesotrophic lakes are geologically middle aged. They are deeper, cooler, and less weedy than eutrophic lakes, but shallower, warmer, and more fertile than oligotrophic lakes. A healthy mesotrophic lake will often

Oligotrophic lakes are characterized by rocky shorelines and clear, infertile water.
SARA KIMM

have a thriving walleye population, with northern pike and, possibly, smallmouth bass. Mesotrophic lakes can be the best muskie lakes—both for numbers and size.

Muskies also thrive in rivers, streams, and reservoirs. And some world record–class muskies are being caught in lakes and river systems connected to the Great Lakes.

There's more. Muskie population size and density factors are partly determined by lake type, as mentioned above. But there are other factors. There are completely wild native muskie populations that are sustained only through natural reproduction and a strong catch-and-release ethic. There are native, naturally reproducing populations that are enhanced with supplemental stockings. And there are stocked muskie populations where there is no reproduction at all, often due to a lack of necessary environmental conditions. These lakes must be maintained through repeated restocking efforts.

In the North Country, a muskie angler can choose to fish originally stocked, but thriving, muskie waters such as Mille Lacs or Lake Vermilion in Minnesota. In recent years these two lakes have been producing 50-pound muskies. Or the same angler can drive another few hundred miles north to fish wild, naturally reproducing muskies in the Canadian Shield lakes of northwest Ontario. Farther east, the Saint Lawrence River, before it enters Lake Ontario, and Georgian Bay, on the northeast side of Lake Huron, have relatively low muskie populations but produce world-record muskies. On the other end of the spectrum (but also connected to the Great Lakes), Lake St. Clair can produce ten muskies or more per day for an experienced charter captain. Picking the water you are going to fish is critical to muskie fishing success or failure.

Another important environmental factor is the day-to-day local weather. Not that weather is always a reliable predictor of muskie behavior. Muskies defy prediction. No single environmental factor is a foolproof predictor. But weather is arguably the most obvious and most consistently cited.

Fishing Pressure

Fishing pressure is not a typical environmental factor, like water quality or local weather, but it is an important one to consider. Think about it. Most wild creatures must be as aware of their natural predators as they are of their natural prey. They have to keep their eyes open—looking both up and down the food chain. A midrange fish species (a perch, for example) must be aware of the muskies, pike, and walleyes above it—just as it is aware of the minnow species it is trying to hunt down and eat. If it wants to stay alive, that perch can't afford to focus completely on little minnows. It has to constantly look back over its shoulder. Is that hungry 36-inch muskie looking at me? Is it moving my way? You get the idea. Perch behavior is influenced by the habits of its prey *and* by the habits of its predators.

Now think about a muskie. Everyone talks about the muskie's prey. Ciscoes, suckers, perch, bullheads … we always want to know, where are the prey? The muskies must be close behind, right? Not so fast. We also need to ask ourselves who are the muskie's predators? What are the muskies looking back over *their* shoulders for? What (or who) presents the biggest danger from above? What? Who? We don't need to look very far. Muskie anglers are the muskie's primary predator.

The Impact of Fishing Pressure

Before you can adapt your strategy to the effects of fishing pressure, you have to ask a few questions. How many muskie anglers fish your lake? How many of them fish your best spots? Is your "milk run" so well known that a lot of people fish the same exact water you do? Do they fish it the same way you do? In the same order? At the same depths? At the same speed? With the same lure types? At the same time of the day?

This may seem like a lot of attention to other anglers' business. But look at it from the muskie's point of view.

If the muskie you want to catch looks for food on the same weedline at the same time every day and is a sucker for fast-moving shiny, spinning blades—and if a few other anglers figure that pattern out—the muskie will see a lot of flashing bucktails at lunch time. There will be follows and figure eights. There will be a chomp into a sharp, stinging "meal" and a quick spit-out. And eventually, there will be a chomp into a sharp, stinging "meal" that the muskie *can't* spit out. There will be an exhausting battle, maybe a slime-scraping net, a rusty pliers in the mouth, the inevitable floating stick with numbers on it, and finally the flashing little box—all before the muskie is freed to swim away. Muskies don't get fat or old repeating that same feeding mode at that time of day on that weedline.

They eventually try another weedline. Or maybe eat at night. And they certainly stop falling for those fast shiny, spinning blades. If they are not able to change their routine, to adapt to the fishing pressure, they will eventually run out of luck.

When that muskie and her buddies do adapt in some way, muskie anglers will start to wonder what happened. Eventually they will start mixing up their routine until they bump into the next effective fishing tactic.

Why wait? Why not get out ahead of the crowd? Why not move away from the conventional before everyone else? The pro muskie angler looks at excessive fishing pressure and doesn't wait for the fishing to get bad. When the pro sees too much fishing pressure, he realizes that it's time to move to something else. Now.

If most anglers are doing the same thing, whether it's fishing a particular piece of structure, fishing at one time of day, or presenting one lure type in one particular way, then you can expect that the muskies will adapt. The really big muskies (usually the shyest) have probably already moved on.

Learn the conventional wisdom on the water you fish. Then go in the opposite direction. Does everyone pound the same obvious spots every day? Then turn your attention to less obvious, even "hidden" spots. Look for structure that may not look perfect to the casual angler. Fish a lot of these secondary spots. When you find an unpressured muskie on one of them, she will not have already been educated. She will not be jaded and bored with bucktails and jerkbaits. Living where she does, on a secondary spot, she hasn't seen very many phony meals. Show her one.

Does everyone else fish the same time of day, let's say afternoons and weekends? Try fishing at the crack of dawn. Does everyone fish weekends on your lake? Take a Wednesday off work. Your muskie may have been conditioned to five days of eating in peace, then two days of harassment, then five more days of eating in peace. Get out there on a peaceful eating day. Does everyone hammer your favorite lake in July and October? Are those two months considered prime time? Take an August vacation. It will be just you and the fish.

What are the preferred presentation styles on your water? What are the regional traditions? Fast retrieves? Slow retrieves? Trolling? Casting? Fishing deep? Shallow? Vertical jigging? Topwater? Sure, that one locally popular presentation must work. It was great in its day, and it still works well enough. But if the muskies see the same presentation day after day, then the susceptible ones will eventually get worn out (and skinny) and the other muskies will have just gotten bored with the same old stuff. Give them something else. At a different speed. At a different depth. At a different angle. Maybe the next big muskie is a sucker for a presentation technique that hasn't been tried yet.

Fishing Presentation "Style"

This is the fun part. It is also the "pro" part.

After looking at all the factors/variables that go into defining a tactic or picking an effective technique for the situation, there is just one last thing to consider: What style of fishing do you enjoy? That may seem like a crazy question. Most folks would say, "I like the style that works. Any style that works is good enough for me." Fair enough. But bear with me. There are two other ways to look at the style question.

There is the question of goals. What is your goal in muskie fishing this coming season? What is your goal on your next trip? What is your goal on the first day of a seven-day trip? What is your goal on the last day of that trip?

The other style issue is philosophical, believe it or not. What is your philosophy about the best *way* to catch a trophy muskie?

First the goals question: One pro fishes tournaments. His goal is to rack up points by catching a number of medium-size muskies in a few days. From big cash tournaments to friendly Muskies, Inc., fund-raisers, there are pros who seem to thrive at the numbers game.

Another pro is a big-fish specialist who focuses on world-class muskies for himself and clients. Marc Thorpe, guide and outdoor writer fishing out of Montreal, is a classic example. Marc can put his clients on multifish muskie days. But that's not his specialty. Marc's specialty is monster muskies. One of his clients caught a 57-incher and a 58-incher in one day. Marc has had a few 50–50 seasons in recent years. That's 50 muskies over 50 inches in one season. I'm not kidding. Marc's numbers are outrageous.

Then there is the philosophical/style question. For example, one pro (lure manufacturer and muskie guide Mark Windels) is famous for his run-and-gun approach. By covering many acres of water per day (but only a thin, two-dimensional slice), Mark connects with many aggressive muskies. For about forty years, a substantial number of Mark's fish have been huge. I first heard of Mark when I read his outstanding articles in the early years of *In-Fisherman* magazine.

Another pro (Lake of the Woods muskie guide, and another *In-Fisherman* contributor, Doug Johnson) prefers to thoroughly and methodically poke and probe a few acres of very good structure, fishing it both shallow and deep (a three-dimensional straining of the entire structure). Doug may contact fewer fish than Mark in an average day, but he catches some big wary monsters that the others miss.

Another philosophical call: What is the best way to deal with all the lake options? So much water, so little time. One idea is to explore and chase. This approach involves constant research and exploration. Sometimes you drive 1,000 miles to fish a lake on a hunch—only to find no muskies … or stunted muskies. Sometimes it's a tip or a rumor, and off you go on a 600-mile wild goose chase … or maybe there's a 57-incher out there that has never seen a muskie lure. It happens.

But there is another way. That approach is to hunker down on one body of water and really learn it. The advantage here is that you have time to learn the secondary unpressured spots. As the world discovers your best spots, you have already moved on to new secondary spots. You also get to stay tuned into the muskies and their environment. If you fish the water frequently enough, you stay "on" the muskies, and they never really get away from you. There are many examples of people who have evolved from the explorer philosophy to the hunker-down philosophy as they got older.

The point here is that pro tactics are sometimes determined by goals, sometimes by philosophy on the best way to catch a big one, and sometimes by the seasonal and environmental variables.

Later in this book, we'll look at techniques and tactics that catch muskies—cutting through the seasonal, environmental, and fishing-style variables that we introduced here. These are the same techniques and tactics that separate the 2 percent from the 98 percent.

CHAPTER THREE

Muskie Fishing Tackle

Few aspects of muskie fishing have evolved as much in recent years as the equipment used to catch them. Light yet durable graphite rods; tough, high-capacity reels; and—perhaps most significantly—no-stretch superlines have all dramatically changed the quality and variety of gear available to muskie anglers.

The number and variety of muskie lures—and the range of techniques they make possible—have grown just as much, if not more.

Sorting through the range of available gear and deciding what's best for you can be a daunting task. Selecting the right gear is a critical part of successful muskie fishing.

Muskie tackle's number-one function is to hook and hold a muskie and allow you to play the fish out so that it can be safely handled and released. More than with any other freshwater game fish, the mechanical integrity of the tackle is critical. There are several reasons for this.

The fish itself is the first reason—its weight, its teeth, its fighting ability, its tendency to strike at boatside when you have a foot or less of line out. Landing a muskie puts tremendous strain on your gear. If there's a weakness in the system—a weak knot, cheap snap or split ring, or bargain-bin reel with a lousy drag—it will be exposed the instant a big muskie is hooked. Not only will you lose a fish you probably worked rather hard at finding and getting to strike but the fish may swim off with a lure pinned in its jaws, and likely die later.

The lures are often huge. Just *fishing* for muskies is tough on gear. It's not uncommon for a fatigued or nicked muskie rod to shatter on the cast. Or for a line to snap, or a reel to seize up, just from the strain of casting a normal muskie lure.

And there is one more sad, but irrefutable, aspect of muskie fishing. You don't get many chances. Compared to panfish, bass, trout, pike, and walleye fishing, opportunities are few and far between—even for the pros. When contact with a muskie is an achievement, when strikes and hookups are precious, tackle failure of any kind is unacceptable.

Muskies require proper equipment, from rods to reels, leader, and line. GREGG THOMAS

Finally, good equipment is a necessity for simply being able to fish effectively. Muskie fishing is often an endurance test. Reels without enough cranking power or rods poorly matched to the lure and technique you're using cause fatigue. Worn-out anglers make mistakes, whether they're mental (not thinking things through) or mechanical (not fishing spots carefully or not seeing a following fish). Or worn-out anglers just head in early. Fatigue will cost you fish, one way or another.

An important thing to consider in gearing up for muskies is the notion of balance. Poorly matched tackle not only keeps you from fishing as effectively as you could, it also just plain takes a lot of the fun out of it. The rod, reel, and line choice must be suited each to the other, and all must be suited for the technique being used. In fact, it's almost impossible to discuss any part of the system in isolation and say anything meaningful.

In this chapter we'll be discussing the components of an effective system for fishing muskies throughout the season, using a variety of techniques.

There's a vast array of muskie gear available. What you need may depend on where and how often you fish. JERRY SONDAG

We'll include not only lure families and how they're used but also the types of rods, reels, line, and leaders necessary to present them effectively and efficiently. In the chapters that follow, as we discuss specific on-the-water tactics, we'll refer back to this discussion frequently.

So how much of this stuff do you really need? It depends on how often you fish and how wide a variety of waters you spend time on. A casual muskie angler who only fishes muskies a few times a year could probably get by with one general-purpose rod and reel combo and a handful of basic lures. Likewise, an angler who fishes primarily one body of water could be very successful with a couple combos and the lures necessary to fish that water effectively.

But if you're going to get serious about things at all, fishing muskies on a variety of waters under a range of conditions and situations, you'll need a broader set of tools. We'll list several lure types and rod and reel combos in the following pages.

A BIT ABOUT ROD ACTION AND LENGTH

Even just a few years ago, a typical muskie rod shared more characteristics with a pool cue that it did with rods used for almost any other species. They were short, often under 6 feet long, and extremely stiff. The prevailing theory was that rods *had* to be short in order to overcome the line stretch of Dacron line and set the hook into a muskie's bony mouth.

Fortunately, rods have evolved a great deal in the last dozen or so years. Today's muskie rod is a far cry from the pool cue of the past. Rods are available in a variety of actions, suited to a range of lure types and presentation techniques. Longer rods with lighter power and faster actions are the norm among most muskie anglers today. Longer rods make casting lures easier, are far more forgiving when fighting fish with no-stretch superlines, and make executing a proper figure eight much easier as well. Simply put, they're far better tools than short, stiff, pool-cue rods.

In general, "longer" and "lighter" describe modern muskie rods, but how we (and rod manufacturers) describe how rods behave can be a little confusing at first. Rods have

two characteristics that describe their behavior: *power* and *action*.

A rod's power is a measurement of how much force or weight is required to bend, or *load*, the blank. A heavy power rod takes significant weight to load the blank, while a light power rod bends fairly easily.

A rod's action (sometimes called the *taper*) describes *where* the blank bends when loaded. Generally speaking, when describing a rod's action, you can divide the rod blank into fourths from top to bottom. A fast-action rod will bend in the top one-fourth of the blank, a medium-action will bend roughly in the middle, while a slow-action will bend nearly to the rod butt. A medium-fast action rod will bend somewhere between the middle and top one-fourth. An extra-fast rod will bend just at the tip, more or less.

The two properties can occur in any combination, and the combining of these properties makes rods function in very different ways. Frankly, it can get a little confusing. So when we describe a fast-action medium-heavy rod, refer back here to see what the heck we mean.

Not all of them may be necessary for you, depending on what types of waters you fish and your fishing style.

Individual preferences vary, so consider the following examples general guidelines. But keep in mind, too, that they're guidelines based on many years on the water and a lot of experimenting with different types of lures, rods, and reels.

Muskie Gear—Rods, Reels, and Lures

Finally, the fun stuff.

Muskie anglers are notorious lure fanatics, constantly adding to their lure collections as they search for the ultimate bait. We're no different. We've acquired thousands over the years.

But lures can get *too much* attention sometimes. To many muskie anglers, lures become an obstacle to catching more muskies, not an aid. Perhaps more than any other group of anglers, muskie anglers are prone to an overemphasis on individual lures or lure styles. They become one-method anglers, doggedly sticking with their favorite lure regardless of conditions. Or they become schizophrenic lure changers, buying new lures by the basket, then changing lures constantly and at random on the water in an endless search for *the* lure—a mystical silver bullet that will catch lots of muskies, all the time—while never bothering to learn what the lures they have actually *do*. Others become so fascinated with the minute details of the lures themselves—so obsessive about the perfect color, just the right action, the indefinable *something* that, in their eyes, makes one lure work better than another—that they forget that lures are actually supposed to be just one part of the puzzle, not an answer in and of themselves.

It's a cliché, but the phrase "lures are just tools" is probably truer when it comes to muskies than any other species. Lures, regardless of style, have a set of characteristics that define their function. For decades, *In-Fisherman* magazine has taught that the way in which lures cause fish to respond to them can be described as a spectrum between two characteristics: attraction and triggering ability. Attraction is the ability to attract a fish's attention and draw it to the lure. Triggering ability is simply the ability to cause a fish to strike, whether from hunger, territorial aggression, curiosity, or just plain predatory instinct and reflexes. Every lure has these two characteristics to

The real objective of lure selection is finding the right tool for the job. MARK HEDIN

greater or lesser degrees, and different situations on the water may call for lures that emphasize different points on that spectrum. Searching for fish scattered across a massive weed flat calls for a lure like a bucktail that can call fish from a distance with flash and vibration. Teasing a strike out of a post–cold front muskie buried in a small pocket of coontail might call for a slow-moving jerkbait that, while not able to call fish in from any distance, can thoroughly strain specific areas and trigger a turned-off fish into striking its erratic, wounded baitfish action.

Now consider the mechanics of how a lure works. For muskies there are three main factors to consider: Speed, running depth, and the ability to fish through cover. How fast or slowly can a lure be fished, and how wide a range of speeds is it capable of? How deep does it run at those speeds? How well—or how poorly—can it be fished around or through cover like weeds, rocks, or wood without hanging up?

Finally, a somewhat subjective factor: hooking ability. Some lures, because of their design, are just plain more efficient at hooking fish than others. For many of the best muskie anglers, hooking ability is the final factor in selecting a lure for a given situation. They ask a simple question: Of the all the lures that I think have the right combination of attraction and triggering for the fish's mood, and that run at the right depth and speed, which one hooks fish the best? When you fish all day for one strike, it only makes sense to give yourself the best chance at actually hooking the thing.

Unfortunately, hooking ability is often a trade-off with other requirements in many situations. The best lure choice might be one that doesn't hook fish particularly well compared to other lure styles. Topwaters are a classic example. In certain situations they can attract and trigger muskies like no other lure, but they're also notoriously poor hookers. But if that's what it takes to fish effectively and get a strike, all you can do is hope for the best.

The point of this whole discussion is this: Lure selection is a purely practical exercise. The goal of lure selection—the *only* goal—is selecting the lure that meets as many of the requirements for the situation (water conditions, time of year, type of cover, depth, fishing pressure, and fish mood) as possible.

The nature of muskie fishing makes this practical approach to lures and lure selection a necessity. Think back to the discussion of the low population density of muskies. Throughout the course of a day, even when fishing's good, you have so few opportunities to contact fish. Choosing a lure because it's this year's hot bait, because it worked yesterday, or last year, or because it's your "favorite lure," can really hurt your odds of catching a muskie. Muskie fishing is a low numbers game in the first place. The odds are already bad enough. Why make it worse?

Topwaters

Up until just a few years ago, topwaters were considered a niche bait by most muskie anglers. They were for calm summer mornings or evenings, and not much else. Fun, certainly—few things are as exciting as a muskie smashing a topwater—but not very versatile compared to other lure types.

Today we know better. Topwaters, used in the right situation, can catch muskies from opening day to ice-up, in a wide range of conditions—even in big waves or frigid late-fall water temperatures. Their broad range of applications makes sense. Muskies have been feeding off the surface since they were fry picking midges and mosquito larva off the surface film. Topwaters also appeal to the opportunistic nature of muskies as predators. Topwaters are suggestive of many things—a distressed and vulnerable surface-swimming *something* that represents an easy meal.

Topwaters, top to bottom: American Hardwoods Lac Seul Turr-bo, Musky Mania Doc, Mouldy's Topper Stopper, Creeper. DAVE OLSON

The surge in popularity of topwaters has led to the introduction of dozens of new models, but though the particulars among individual baits vary, most of them are derived from a few basic styles: tail- or head-spinning propbaits (sometimes called "pop-pop" baits for the loud and distinct popping sound the blade makes when retrieved), subtle propbaits, walk-the-dog stickbaits, and creepers or wobblers.

Tail- or head-spinning pop-pop topwaters like the Pacemaker (a tail-spinning bait) or the Holcombe Tackle's Tsunami (a head-spinning bait) are perhaps the style of bait that led to the renaissance of topwaters for muskies. These baits are often fairly loud and can call fish from a distance, even in 3-foot waves. On some of Minnesota's large muskie lakes, tail-spinning topwaters in wind over shallow reefs and weed flats have accounted for some huge muskies.

Baits of this type can be fished fairly quickly, with a steady retrieve, making them good search lures for covering large spots like large reefs or flats. Most also have a fairly broad speed range, allowing you to speed up your retrieve when a following fish is spotted. Though simply casting them out and reeling them straight in will get you bit, varying the speed throughout your retrieve can be a good way to trigger more strikes with these baits.

At the other end of the sound spectrum from pop-pop baits are subtle propbaits like the Mouldy's Topper Stopper. These baits have small prop blades at the front and back of the lure body, and are often fairly small baits overall. The body of a Topper Stopper, minus the blades, is all of about 4 inches long. Not very big, as muskie lures go.

While pop-pop baits create a distinct staccato popping sound, propbaits are more subdued, producing a steady buzz. Propbaits are among the oldest of muskie topwater styles, but they're also still among the most underused. They're extraordinarily versatile—a true all-season bait. Despite their subtle sound and relatively small size, they're even effective in heavy waves.

Propbaits have a fairly broad speed range, so they're good search lures for covering large areas. They're also, because they're a little subtler than pop-pop baits, a good choice for colder water or tougher conditions when fish may not chase a more aggressive bait.

One final note on this style of bait is the apparent importance of sound. Propbaits like Topper Stoppers simply seem to work better if, along with the splashing from the blades, the blades squeak on the lure's wire shaft as they spin. Fans of this bait style get nearly fanatical about having the "right" sound and will sort through several of them before finding one that sounds right—at least to them. Most of these baits seem to get louder as they get worn from use. Roughing up the wire shaft where the blades spin with sandpaper can help, and some anglers speed up the breaking-in process by hanging the bait from their truck antenna as they drive to the lake. (We're serious!) Sometimes it helps, but, in the end, some baits "have it" and some don't. Only time and use will tell you. But if you get a new propbait, and you can hear it squeaking when it's 40 feet from the boat, hang on to it. Better yet, send it to us, and we'll hang on to it for you.

Walk-the-dog-style baits like the Musky Mania Doc and American Hardwood Lures' J-Walker are outsized versions of the classic bass topwater, the Zara Spook. Working this style of lure is a learned skill and can take some practice. Start by reeling slowly and steadily, then gently tapping the rod tip downwards 4 to 5 inches as you reel. Different models require different amounts of length and force on the twitches to get the bait walking, so you'll need to experiment.

Walk-the-dog topwaters can be tremendously effective at attracting and triggering muskies at times. There's something nearly magical about the steady side-to-side action of these baits that can call fish up. But they have their drawbacks. Most can't be fished very fast, making them most effective when fishing small areas or as throwback baits to areas where you know a fish is located because it followed another lure, rather than as search lures. They can often be famously poor hooking baits, eliciting spectacular blowups with lots of excitement and flying water, but no fish.

Most lures of this type also have a fairly limited speed range. Work them too fast and they stop gliding, or pop out of the water altogether. With a limited speed range, triggering following fish can be a challenge. Two common methods of triggering following fish are slowing the reel speed down while continuing to work the lure, making the lure nearly walk in place in front of a following fish, or adding shaper twitches into the retrieve to make the bait dart erratically, imitating a fleeing baitfish.

Creeper- or wobbler-style topwaters are another old and popular lure style. These lures wobble, paddle, and churn across the surface at a slow, steady pace and have accounted for a lot of big muskies over the years. Examples of this style include the Musky Buster Wave Walker and the classic Mouldy's Hawg Wobbler.

Lures of this type usually have one speed—slow. It's a drawback when it comes to covering water, but these lures more than make up for it with their ability to draw strikes when used to fish small areas or when returning to fish that have followed other lures. Returning at dark to a big fish, and throwing a slow-moving creeper or Hawg Wobbler is a classic tactic that has accounted for many, many big muskies over the years. Creepers are also probably the best hooking of any topwater style. While walk-the-dog topwaters and pop-pop baits can draw spectacular strikes, and lots of missed fish, muskies—even huge ones—will often take a creeper with hardly a ripple. The slow, steady, straight-line retrieve makes them an easy target, and muskies just swim up and eat the things.

Rods and Reels for Topwaters

Topwaters usually aren't terribly large, or particularly heavy, so most muskie anglers throw them on rods in the 7- to 8-foot range, with a fast-action and medium to medium-heavy power. Smaller topwaters like Topper Stoppers or other small propbaits can usually be worked with a heavy bass-style flipping stick. Longer rods like 7-foot, 6-inch and 8-foot rods can help steer topwaters around cover, help increase casting distance, and, most important, help you zigzag or change your lure's direction when you spot following fish. With longer rods you can also perform better figure eights at boatside.

The one exception to the preference for long rods is walk-the-dog style lures. Anglers who work these baits by driving the rod tip straight down often prefer shorter rods to keep the rod tip from slapping the water. So rods in the 6½- to 7-foot range may work better for some.

Reels for topwaters can cover a range of options. Topwaters usually don't pull particularly hard; so high-power, low gear ratio reels aren't a necessity—though they'll obviously work fine. Midsize casting reels like the Ambassadeur 6600EXT or Shimano Calcutta 400b balance well with slightly lighter rods used for topwaters. Gear ratio isn't critical with topwaters, though walk-the-dog baits can be easier to work with high-speed reels (6.3:1 gear ratio) that can pick up slack quickly. The same reels work well with flipping sticks. You can also pair a flipping stick with a heavy-duty low-profile reel like a Shimano Curado 300DSV.

AMERICAN HARDWOOD LURES

One particular family of topwater lures deserves mention. We have never seen muskie lures tougher than these—or better designed. For their construction quality alone, these lures are worth a look.

They are all built with true through-wire construction, so you don't have to worry about screw eyes getting loose and coming out. All hooks are connected to the main wire shaft, which is closed at both ends. The only way to remove the hooks from the shaft is to cut the wire with a bolt cutter. Paint jobs are protected by two thick coats of epoxy. All lures are hand-tuned and tank tested. Check out their Web site at www.musky-lures.com.

American Hardwood lures, top to bottom: Lac Seul Mini, Lac Seul Turr-bo, Lac Seul Giant, Ti-Foon, Kry-Bay-Be, J-Walker, Giant Klunker, and Two Timer. DAVE OLSON

Bucktails

There are few things about muskie fishing you can say with certainty. But it's a certainty that more muskies have been caught on in-line bucktails than any other type of lure. In-line bucktails for muskies can be traced back at least as far as the 1880s, and they have been a fundamental tool of muskie anglers ever since.

"Bucktail," it should be said, is a generic term from the deer tail used to create skirts on many of these lures. But skirt material can range from actual bucktail to living rubber or silicone, feathers like chicken hackle or marabou, and even flashy tinsel, Flashabou, or other synthetic fibers.

Bucktails have many qualities and characteristics that make them good muskie lures. The flashing blades and vibration can attract muskies from a distance, and they can be fished quickly to efficiently cover water. They have a broad speed range, so they're not only versatile under a variety of conditions but you can use their speed range to trigger following fish. They figure-eight exceptionally well. They hook fish exceptionally well, too. Beneath the skirt of a bucktail, there's not much for a fish to clamp down on but hooks.

As a family of lures, bucktails can be divided further into a few basic styles. The distinctions are a little arbitrary, but generally you can divide bucktails by bait size and speed range. Of course, it's possible to fish almost any bucktail at any speed, but large baits with big blades pull harder than most anglers are willing to tolerate when fished at anything faster than a moderate pace. There's a very real distinction between what's possible and what's practical. Speed is also an important factor in selecting the right bucktail for the situation. At times, a small, fast-moving bucktail might be ideal for covering water quickly or for attracting and triggering active, aggressive muskies. In other situations, a large profile bait with a big, thumping blade fished more slowly might be a better choice.

In-line bucktails, top to bottom: Blue Fox Vibrax Musky Buck, Musky Mania Lilly Tail, Shumway Flasher, Windels Harasser, Northland Bionic Bucktail. DAVE OLSON

Baits like the Blue Fox Musky Buck or Windels Muskie Harasser are good examples of small to mid-size, relatively compact bucktails. With #7 French blades (the Musky Buck) or larger willowleaf blades (the Harasser), these baits can be fished fast without wearing you out, cast easily, and are excellent hooking baits. In many situations, speed is an important triggering tool for muskies, and bucktails like these are unmatched for their ability to be fished fast and efficiently.

On the other end of the spectrum from small, fast-moving baits like the Musky Buck are large-bodied, large-bladed bucktails like the Eagle Tail. These baits often have thickly tied bucktail skirts and large, fluted Indiana or Colorado blades that pull hard but produce a heavy thump and lots of flash when retrieved at slow to moderate speeds. Double-bladed models like the Shumway Magnum Flasher and the Musky Mayhem Cowgirl are a relatively new phenomenon in large bucktails. The double blades (often #10 Colorado blades) and marabou or Flashabou skirts on these baits create a huge profile in the water—they're definitely a big fish bait.

Large bucktails can be extremely effective when fished slowly over the tops of weedbeds or reefs, during cold-water periods late in the season, in heavy wind and waves where the large profile and loud vibration help fish locate the bait, and at night.

A final type of bucktail worth mentioning is the bulger bucktail. Bulgers are typically lightly weighted and are often tied with marabou or living rubber to help them cast better, despite their lack of additional weight. Bulgers like the Shumway Flasher and Musky Mania Lilly Tail are

CREDIT WHERE CREDIT IS DUE: MARK WINDELS

Seldom does one particular bait change the landscape of an entire sport. But a case can be made for the Windels Harasser having that kind of effect on muskie fishing. In many ways, the Harasser, and the man who makes it, Minnesota muskie angler and lure manufacturer Mark Windels, helped usher in the modern era of muskie fishing. In a series of articles in the *In-Fisherman* in the early 1980s, Windels detailed his systematic approach to muskie fishing—a high-efficiency search for active, aggressive fish on prominent pieces of shallow structure. At a time when most articles about muskies treated them as mysterious, near-mythical creatures, Windels's practical, pragmatic approach was groundbreaking. Along with the system itself, these articles included some of the first mentions of high-capacity reels like the Ambassadeur 7000, descriptions of how to make high-quality steel leaders, techniques for executing a proper figure eight, and the advantages of longer, softer, fast-action rods over short pool-cue muskie rods. The system Windels described influenced a generation of muskie anglers and is still a fundamental approach to catching muskies.

The Windels Harasser—a fundamental of modern muskie fishing. DAVE OLSON

made with either single or double Colorado blades, which create a lot of lift on the retrieve. The combination of light weight and high lift keeps bulgers at or near the surface at all but the slowest speeds, where they create a wake or "bulge" as the blades nearly or just barely break the surface film. Bulgers can be exciting—and very effective—when fished over thick weedbeds or shallow reefs and are excellent throwback bait for fish that have followed other lures. Though their size places them in the big-bait category, many of the super-magnum double-bladed bucktails like Shumway's Magnum Flasher and the Cowgirl are derivatives of the bulger family.

Rods and Reels for Bucktails

Nowhere is the trend toward longer, lighter power, faster action rods more pronounced than in bucktail rods. Medium to medium-light power, fast-action rods in the 7-foot, 6-inch to 8-foot, 6-inch range are typical for bucktails like Musky Bucks, Harassers, or small to midsize bulger bucktails. Lighter power, faster action rods load far better on the cast with light to medium-size baits in the 1- to 2½-ounce range and are less fatiguing than stiffer rods that require pure arm strength to muscle cast lighter baits. Fatigue is a factor in reel choice too. At first glance, high-speed reels would seem to make sense for bucktails, especially for fishing them fast. But high-speed reels have far less cranking power than lower gear ratio reels, and even small-bladed bucktails can wear an angler out when you're cranking them at high speed all day. Wide-spooled, low-gear-ratio reels like the Ambassadeur 7000 are definitely the ideal for bucktails. Larger bucktails, and especially the super-magnum baits like Magnum Flashers or Cowgirls require a heavier rod—less for working the bait than for simply casting them. Heavy power, fast to medium-fast action rods in the 7- to 8-foot range work well for big bucktails.

Jerkbaits

Jerkbaits are muskie lures that demand something of the angler. Wood or plastic, shaped like a shad, a small baseball bat, or a rounded-off length of 1x2 pine board, jerkbaits have little or no built-in action. Everything a jerkbait does in the water, every move the bait makes, is imparted by the angler in the form of jerks, twitches, or pulls of the rod.

There are two main families of jerkbaits: dive-and-rise baits like the Suick (top) and glide baits like the Fudally Reef Hawg (bottom). DAVE OLSON

Even though there are hundreds of models, there are two basic styles: dive and rise, and gliders. Divers (sometimes called "chop-style" jerkbaits) dive on the jerk and, unless weighted, tend to float up between jerks. The Suick is one classic example of a dive-and-rise jerkbait. Gliders move side to side in a walk-the-dog action when retrieved with frequent taps or jerks of the rod. The Reef Hawg is a typical glider.

Divers are an all-season muskie lure. You can work them fast or slow, shallow or deep (if weighted). But one place divers produce surprisingly well is fished over weedy flats. Diver jerkbaits can be driven down into weed pockets and lanes, and will almost back themselves out of a weed patch on the rise. With the right touch, a diver can be coaxed through nearly any weedbed. A lot of experienced muskie anglers will reach for Suick when they want to fish through a weedbed. The slow jerk-and-pause pattern necessary to navigate through a weedbed produces ferocious strikes.

Gliders can also be worked fast or slow, but because of their side-to-side zigzag action, they are not very effective in heavy weeds. The name of our example—the Reef Hawg—serves as a reminder that gliders are at their best fished over rocks and reefs. In warm water, when the muskies are amped up, a fairly rapid tap-tap-tap on the rod and the resultant rhythmic zigzag action of the lure produce powerful "self-setting" strikes. In colder water, when the muskies are less eager to chase, a very slow pull and lethargic lure action give the appearance of an easy meal.

Most jerkbaits are buoyant floaters that pop to the surface on the stop or pause. So they are not considered deep runners. Many anglers add weight to some of their jerkbaits to get them to sink on the pause so they will run deep. And some add just enough weight so that the lure is neutrally buoyant—it neither sinks nor pops to the surface, but hovers in place on the pause. Most weighting techniques involve drilling holes in the lure's belly and using epoxy to secure sinkers in the holes. A simpler way is to attach a bell sinker to the front hook hanger. Some jerkbaits, including Suicks, are sold in both weighted and unweighted models.

There is a lot of conversation out there about how to work a jerkbait. The length of the pull—from a long sideways sweep to a short downward tap-tap-tap of the rod tip is—is one thing everyone has an opinion on. The speed of retrieve and frequency of jerks is another. The only way to learn what works for you is to try them out. The action of the lure—how it shimmies and shakes, how it comes through the weeds, how it triggers strikes—will tell you how you should work your jerkbaits.

This happens every day somewhere in the muskie fishing world: A novice will be experimenting, trying out different jerkbait moves, and will ask a veteran if his technique looks OK. The veteran will look into the water at the novice's lure darting and lurching in a way that the veteran (and most muskies) has never seen before. The veteran will then mutter, "Whatever you are doing, keep doing it." And you know what happens next: Some wild-eyed muskie comes roaring up and validates the veteran's opinion. There are few wrong ways to work a jerkbait.

Rods and Reels for Jerkbaits

There was a time when the phrase "jerkbait rod" meant the typical pool-cue rod of the bad old days—5½ feet long, with very little flex. Times have changed. A 7-foot length became standard in the early '90s. Today, with many people using muskie casting rods in the 8- to 9-foot range, 7-footers are starting to look short and stubby again. With jerkbaits, where rod movement and control is vital, we think there is a limit.

For diver jerkbaits, a 7-foot, 6-inch rod in a medium to medium-heavy power is ideal. For glider jerkbaits, a 7-foot rod in a medium-heavy power is better. Why the difference? There are a few factors. Divers are often lighter in weight, so you will need a slightly longer rod to cast them easily. Also, gliders are often finessed through weedbeds. A longer rod helps you steer the lure around moss, ribbon grass, and other obstacles you want to avoid. Gliders are often heavier, so they cast like a bullet. You don't need a long rod to fire them into a wind. But the most important reason we limit glider rod length to 7 feet is because we often work the bait with the rod pointing down at the six o'clock position and move it with fairly rapid straight-down taps. This is difficult from most boats with rods longer than 7 feet.

With jerkbait fishing, your reel rapidly takes up slack line created when you pull the lure toward you. Too much slack line, and you will miss fish. A powerful high-speed reel like the Ambassadeur 7000 HSN, the Shimano Calcutta 400B, or the standard Ambassadeur 7000 (slower speed, but great line pickup due to the large spool diameter) will all do the job.

Spinnerbaits

Muskie spinnerbaits are not as traditional as jerkbaits, in-line bucktails, or spoons. They came out of the bass-fishing world in the 1970s—at least in terms of popularity—and quickly built a loyal following in the muskie world. A handful of old traditionalists still don't "get" spinnerbaits. "They don't represent any muskie food source, so why would a muskie strike them?" Others are so enamored with spinnerbaits that during certain times of year, they snap one on in the morning and change lures only when the first one wears out. Seriously, even some fishing book authors do this.

First let's dispense with the question: "Why would a muskie strike such a goofy-looking thing?" No one knows why. Who knows how a muskie "thinks"? But the evidence is in. After nearly forty years of use and many thousands of muskies caught, spinnerbaits have proven that muskies strike them.

But muskies strike a lot of lure concoctions. Spinnerbaits are popular with the people who love them because they are so versatile. Because they are essentially a jig with one or more spinning blades to keep them from dropping too quickly, they can be fished at any depth, from top to bottom. Spinnerbaits can be retrieved at any speed, from barely subsurface to slowly

Spinnerbaits, top to bottom: Shumway Funky Chicken, Ruff Tackle Rad Dog, CJ's. DAVE OLSON

crawled along with the blade barely thumping (this is called "slow-rolling"). But that's not all. Spinnerbaits are as weedless and snagless as anything short of a Texas-rigged plastic worm. They can be retrieved through weeds, reeds, lily pads, and bulrushes. They can be dragged over stumps, rocks, and boulders. The spinnerbait is easily the most versatile muskie lure there is. Dick Pearson, whom you may have seen in *In-Fisherman* or *The Next Bite—Esox Angler* magazine, has said: "Lures are tools, and the spinnerbait is the crescent wrench of lures—adjustable to any need."

Many spinnerbaits have a tied deer hair (bucktail) body. CJ's Spinnerbait is a high-quality example of the bucktail-style spinnerbait. As with in-line bucktails, other body materials—such as living rubber or silicone, marabou and chicken feathers, and Mylar tinsel and Flashabou—offer a "breathing," lifelike action. These baits are easier to cast because the body material mats up when wet, so it doesn't catch the air like deer hair. The Rad Dog has a rubber-skirted body, with feathers and Mylar strips for flash and the appearance of volume. Shumway's Funky Chicken spinnerbaits have a marabou body, with a few chicken feathers for bulk.

The configuration and size of the blades is a more important factor than body material. Larger blades and multiple blades add lift so that a spinnerbait will ride high in the water at slower speeds. Smaller blades and single blades have less lift and are better suited to fishing deeper. The most versatile setup is probably a single #7 or # 8 Colorado blade on a 1- to 2-ounce spinnerbait. The single Colorado blade gives you enough lift to bring the lure up shallow at moderate speeds, and it has enough thump to telegraph the lure's status back to the angler's hands—even down deep and at the slowest speeds. It's that telegraphic thump of the blade that keeps you constantly tuned in to the lightest push-type muskie strike. When the thumping stops, set the hook.

A NOTE ON LURE COLORS

As with all other lure characteristics, color is a factor in lure selection. But it is not one to obsess about. Compared to the other factors we've mentioned—action, running depth, and speed of retrieve—color comes in a distant fourth in importance. At best. That said, a case can be made for color at least being a minor consideration. Color selection for muskies is not a finely tuned science. It can't be—your sample size is too small. Most days you're hard pressed to identify a preference between bucktails or jerkbaits, much less particular color shades. The best you can do is choose colors based on a couple of basic principles.

Most of the arguments about color can be distilled down to two schools of thought. One side says that a lure works best when its color pattern matches the color of a primary baitfish in the body of water. A color's ability to imitate, or at least suggest, the muskie's natural forage is the objective. The other side says that a lure works best when its color contrasts with the hue of the water, making the lure easier to see. Thus, the color's visibility is the important thing.

Both sides are right. Rather, they are each right some of the time. On crystal-clear oligotrophic lakes—especially when there is a bright sun—lures are very easy to see. Visibility is not a challenge. But phoniness may be. It's not that muskies are smart and able to recognize danger in an unnatural-looking lure. It's just that they can see it so easily and from so far away that they have time to reject a gaudy lure because it is neither food nor threat. In this situation, a more natural color may fool the fish for a while—sneak up on it, if you will—and startle it so that it strikes out of reflex.

But when you fish a fertile mesotrophic lake in August when there is a thick algae bloom, getting the fish's attention and providing a visible target is your challenge. To achieve visibility in the green water, bright colors and, perhaps more important, high-contrast color combinations like an orange-and-black lure may be better, despite being "unnatural." As the lure passes a few feet from a muskie, the fish can barely make it out. Even this loud color combination is barely visible. It passes the fish as a shadow in the murk. Food or threat? Either way, at least you have a chance.

A middle ground between these two approaches is also possible by considering pattern and contrast. If the main forage in a body of water is yellow perch, you can attempt to imitate it with a natural perch pattern. A lure with the same general pattern—dark vertical bars with lighter yellow or green in between—but with increased contrast and intensity, like solid black bars and fluorescent-green sides, can suggest the forage but increase your lure's visibility.

Color is also a way to combat fishing pressure. If everyone knows that you are supposed to troll pink and purple crankbaits on Lake XYZ, then maybe the muskies are getting conditioned to pink and purple. Maybe the muskies see so much pink and purple that those colors have lost their ability to produce strikes. When you troll that lake, try gold and brown crankbaits. Sometimes, simply being different is enough.

Rods and Reels for Spinnerbaits

For casting spinnerbaits, a 7-foot, 6-inch to 8-foot rod in a medium to medium-heavy power is usually about right for lures in the ¾- to 2½-ounce range. For lighter spinnerbaits sometimes used in cold springtime waters, an 8-foot medium-power muskie rod, or even a heavy bass rod, paired with a low-profile reel like a Shimano Curado 300DSV or a traditional midsize muskie reel like the Ambassadeur 6600EXT will make casting easier. For spinnerbaits 3 ounces and larger, you will want to beef up to a 7-foot, 6-inch to 8-foot rod in a heavy power.

For all muskie-size spinnerbaits (1 ounce or more), especially those with larger blades, you DO NOT want to use a reel with a high gear ratio. Large-bladed spinnerbaits can pull like a mule. A low gear ratio reel trades away speed in favor of power. It's power that takes the work out of retrieving a lure. The best spinnerbait reel is an Ambassadeur 7000i with a 4.1:1 gear ratio.

Crankbaits

Crankbaits are the easiest lures to understand when you look at them. They are often shaped like a baitfish, so no questions about why a muskie would strike them. They have a diving lip or body shape that imparts action when you reel them in. At their most basic, all you have to do is cast them out and crank them in. Hence the name. But crankbaits can be fished a number of other ways. They are often trolled—in fact, many crankbaits were originally designed as trolling lures. And like jerkbaits, crankbaits can be retrieved in any combination of twitches, jerks, and pauses.

Crankbaits come in a multitude of styles and running depths.

Minnow baits have a lip style like an original Rapala. The size, shape, and angle of the diving lip dictates, to a large degree, the running depth and intensity of action of these types of crankbaits.

A very popular and effective minnow-style bait is the Jake from Drifter Tackle. Jakes range in size from tiny 6-inch finesse baits to 14-inch monsters that we hope are intended for trolling only. Jakes are designed for all possible crankbait purposes: trolling, cranking, and twitching/ripping. The popular 10-inch Jake can be trolled 6 to 20 feet deep, depending on the amount of line out. Another minnow-style bait that is ideal for early-season finesse twitching is the Bomber Long-A.

Deep-diver crankbaits, like the Ernie and the Depth Raider, have a lip angle that drives the lure into deeper water. Deep-diver crankbaits can be straight-cranked or twitched. But their special niche is deep water. Depending on lip design and line length, deep divers can be effectively trolled 20 to 40 or more feet deep.

Banana-style crankbaits like the Believer have no lip, but instead achieve their action and diving ability from the curved shape of the body and the connection point. Believers have two front eyelets—connection points for snapping on your leader. The eyelet closer to the nose of the lure is for shallow running (and for fishing through weeds). The eyelet farther back is for deep running. These baits were originally designed for trolling on Lake St. Clair but were eventually discovered to be excellent casting bait—especially when fishing through weedbeds. These lures can be trolled 8 to 22 feet deep.

Crankbaits are also available with soft plastic tails that add a lifelike action, even at very slow speeds. The Shallow Invader from Muskie Innovations is designed as a shallow-running twitch bait. The action tail is especially effective when the lure is fished slowly, with dead pauses . . . deadly pauses, that is.

Crankbaits, top to bottom: Musky Mania Jake, Bomber Long-A, Bucher Depth Raider, Musky Mania Lil' Ernie, Musky Innovations Shallow Invader, Drifter Tackle Believer. DAVE OLSON

Rods and Reels for Crankbaits

Rods and reels for crankbaits are not much different from those used for spinnerbaits. The larger, hard-diving crankbaits require a 7-foot, 6-inch to 8-foot rod in a heavy power, paired with an Ambassadeur 7000 with a 4.1:1 gear ratio. The shallower running, easier pulling crankbaits will work better with a 7-foot, 6-inch to 8-foot rod in a medium to medium-heavy power and a high-speed reel like the Ambassadeur 7000i HSN or the Shimano Calcutta 400B. Of course, if you drop down to light 6-inch finesse/twitch baits, then an 8-foot medium power or a heavy bass flipping stick with a Shimano Curado 300DSV or 6000 series Ambassadeur reel will work.

Spoons

The oldest, most proven—and yet most underappreciated—lures in muskie fishing are spoons. Yes, lowly spoons. Spoons were probably the first artificials to catch large numbers of pike and muskies. To this day, spoons just flat out catch fish. For muskies, spoons are very effective when fished erratically, twitched and jerked and allowed to flutter on the drop. There is no wrong way to work a spoon. And spoons are easy to cast and retrieve.

The Eppinger Dardevle has been doing it for over one hundred years. But Len Thompson spoons and larger Red Eye Wigglers offer similar strike-provoking actions.

For fishing in heavy weeds, a large weedless Johnson Silver Minnow, with a plastic or pork rind trailer, cannot be beat. The thickest slop that stops all other lures is no match for a weedless spoon.

Spoons, clockwise from top: Dardevle, Pro-Scale weedless spoon, Len Thompson, Johnson's Silver Minnow. DAVE OLSON

Rods and Reels for Spoons

Spoons are easy to cast and offer little resistance on the retrieve. They can be comfortably thrown with rods in the 7- to 8-foot range, with a fast action and medium to medium-heavy power. Midsize casting reels like the Ambassadeur 6500c or Shimano Calcutta 400B balance well with these rods. In other words, spoons can be handled with your topwater and lighter bucktail rods and reels.

Jigs and Soft Plastics

Jigs and soft plastics are another curious case when it comes to muskies. It's a lure family that is at once old and new. Jigging for muskies with classic lead-head jigs has enjoyed pockets of regional popularity for decades without catching on with the wider muskie-fishing public, while using large soft plastic swimbaits and giant tubes are relatively recent developments that have caught on in a big way.

Jigs like the Bait Rigs Esox Cobra jig are perhaps one of the most overlooked presentations for muskies. Jigs are extraordinarily versatile. They can be fished at virtually any depth, from just below the surface down to the bottom in 30 feet of water. Their speed range is nearly as broad. They can be fished vertically or horizontally—or some of each on a single cast. Jigs have little inherent action of their own. How the lure behaves— its speed, running depth, and action—are all dependent on the angler.

Good muskie jigs have a few common traits. Since they are primarily casting lures, the line tie should be forward on the jig so that the weight of the head is behind and below the line tie, not centered beneath it as on typical round-head jigs. A quality hook is critical. Esox Cobra jigs, for example, have wide-gap Mustad UltraPoint hooks. Fiber weed guards are common on a lot of muskie jigs on the market but frankly aren't necessary in all but the thickest cover. For most situations your hooking percentage will increase if you cut the weed guard off—or at the very least, trim it significantly.

Jigs are usually paired with some sort of soft plastic. A classic example is a swimming head jig like an Esox Cobra, and an 8-inch Reaper tail.

Jigs and soft plastics, top to bottom: Red October Tube, Musky Mayhem Stick 'Em Jig, Musky Innovations Bull Dawg, Bait Rigs Esox Cobra Jig. DAVE OLSON

This combination can be fished along deep weedlines and over deep rocks with a sharp lift-fall retrieve, or a steady swimming retrieve with occasional pauses to let the jig and Reaper flutter and swim downward. Another effective combination is to add a silicone or living rubber skirt to the jighead, along with a large shad body like a 6-inch Lunker City Salt Shaker. The combination of a fluttering skirt and thumping shad tail is deadly fished horizontally over the tops of weedbeds or rock reefs. The jig/shad body combination casts exceptionally well and can be fished quickly to cover water with a steady retrieve broken by brief pauses to let the jig dart and flutter downward.

Soft plastic swimbaits like the Musky Innovations Bull Dawg are another jig-type option for muskies. In many ways they're a bait style so different they're almost a family all their own. These large, action-tail soft plastics are, at least in terms of how they're used, hybrid baits that combine traits of both jerkbaits and more traditional jigs. Ranging in sizes from small, 6-inch models to outsized versions that are 16 inches long and weigh in at a pound and change, Bull Dawgs can be applied to a range of situations. Methods for working Bull Dawgs and similar swimbaits are equally broad. They can be twitched like jerkbaits, ripped aggressively, jigged, or simply reeled straight in. They're a bait that's hard to fish wrong. Smaller versions are excellent early-season or post–cold front baits, while larger models can be used all season and excel in cold water after turnover.

Along with action-tail swimbaits, giant tube baits are a fairly new development in the muskie world. Giant-size versions of the popular bass lure, tubes like the Red October from Red October Baits can be rigged on jigheads or fished weightless on large single hooks with a trailing treble. As when fished for bass, tubes are quite versatile, imitating nothing in particular, but with a gliding, fluttering action that definitely triggers even reluctant fish. Giant tubes are fairly new at the time of this writing, so exactly how and when they're best used is a story that remains to be written.

Rods and Reels for Jigs and Plastics

Rod and reel choice for jigs and plastics varies widely depending on specific lure type.

For jigs like the Esox Cobra, whether with a Reaper tail or skirt and shad body, light to medium-light, fast action rods in the 7-foot, 6-inch to 8-foot range, like the Shimano Crucial Swimbait rod, or heavy bass-flipping sticks are good choices. In many cases, rod lengths and actions similar to light bucktail rods work well. Match them with a 6000 series Ambassadeur, a Shimano Calcutta 400, or Shimano Curado 300DSV.

Bull Dawgs, heavier jigs, and heavily weighted tubes can require significantly heavier tackle; 7 foot to 8 foot medium-heavy to heavy power rods for standard size Bull Dawgs, and X-heavy or XX-heavy power rods for magnum versions. High capacity, low gear ratio reels like the Ambassadeur 7000 handle the weight of heavy lures like Bull Dawgs well.

Trolling Gear

Trolling for muskies requires a somewhat different set of gear than casting. Trolling rods are typically long and often have much slower actions than casting rods. Slow actions absorb some of the pressure of hard-pulling lures and, more important, absorb some of the shock when a muskie hits, especially when rods are placed in rod holders. A 30-pound muskie hitting a lure being trolled at 4 miles per hour isn't a strike—it's a collision. Troll with rods that are too stiff, and at best you'll pull the hooks out of the fish; at worst, something—rod, line, leader, or rod holder—will simply break. Softer rod tips also help trolled lures bounce out of snags when trolling around rocks. Many hard-core trollers also prefer fiberglass over graphite, simply because of its durability.

For trolling crankbaits like Jakes, Depth Raiders, or Believers, rods in the 7-foot, 6-inch to 9-foot, 6-inch range with medium-heavy to heavy power and medium to medium-fast actions work well. Long rods, sometimes up to 10 feet, help spread lines when trolling with several lines in the water.

Many muskie anglers have found that relatively inexpensive Great Lakes trolling rods like the Shimano Talora series Dipsey Diver rods are economical, effective muskie trolling rods for pulling crankbaits, either on flat lines or behind planer boards.

Spinnerbait and jerkbait trolling takes slightly different equipment. Much of the time spinnerbaits and jerkbaits are trolled over and around weed growth, and rods need to be stiff enough to rip the lure free of the weeds, rather than just pulling the weeds free of the stalk, which fouls

Line-counter reels with smooth drags like the Shimano Tekota 600LC filled with low-stretch superline are excellent for trolling. DAVE OLSON

the lure. Rods for these techniques are similar to a heavy bucktail rod—medium-heavy to heavy power, with a medium-fast to fast action.

Trolling reels have one primary requirement: a smooth drag. Drags that slip unpredictably or, worse yet, grab and lock up when a fish hits, can lead to disaster. In most cases, your drag tension should be set fairly light so that fish can take line freely while you pull a rod out of a rod holder. Line-counter reels aren't a necessity—you can get an approximation of how much line is out by counting passes of the reel's level wind. But if you plan on doing much trolling at all, line counters are definitely recommended. Especially when trolling tight to structure, or when targeting open-water fish at a specific depth, lure running depth can be critical, and running depth is a function of how much line is out. Line counters allow precise measurement of line out and, more important, allow you to quickly and accurately repeat setups that worked. Both of us have found that the Shimano Tekota 600LC is an exceptional muskie trolling reel, with a silky-smooth drag and a reliable line-counter system that functions even in subzero weather late in the season.

Lines and Leaders

We could easily have begun the discussion of tackle and equipment with line. The advent of no-stretch "superlines" made from Spectra or Microdyneema fibers in the early 1990s has had a huge effect on muskie tackle, especially rod design and actions. The total lack of stretch has made the switch to longer, softer rods a virtual necessity for most techniques. With zero-stretch line and a traditional short, pool-cue rod, there's no give at all in the system. Hooks simply pull out of hooked fish.

Superlines in the 80- to 100-pound-test category, like Cortland Spectron or Cortland Master Braid are the line of choice for nearly all muskie techniques. These lines are extraordinarily durable, often lasting several seasons before needing to be replaced (a fact that makes the initial price a lot easier to swallow). Many beginning muskie anglers balk at lines in the 60- to 100-pound-test range, opting for line in the 35- to 40-pound-test range. This is usually a mistake.

Obviously, muskies don't get big enough to break 100-pound test. A more important property than break strength, though, is line diameter. Eighty-pound superline is roughly similar in diameter to 30- or 36-pound Dacron, the standard muskie line before superlines came on the scene. Line of this diameter performs far better on large baitcasting reels than smaller diameter line, and is far less prone to digging into the spool if you backlash on a cast. Break strength, though, *does* matter if you backlash with a heavy muskie lure. Consider the physics involved in casting a large muskie lure with zero-stretch line. A 6-ounce lure, being driven by an 8-foot rod, that stops short on a backlash can generate far more force than zero-stretch 35-pound test can handle, as many new superline users have discovered when their favorite (probably fairly expensive) lure flies over the horizon on a minor backlash. Stick with the heavier stuff.

Although superlines are the right choice for the vast majority of situations and techniques, monofilament still has a place. Twenty- to 30-pound mono like Berkley Trilene XT or Big Game matches well with a flipping stick for topwaters, small crankbaits, and jigs. The shock-absorbing ability of mono is extremely forgiving when fighting fish on lighter tackle. The shock-absorbing stretch of mono can also be an advantage when trolling, especially over open water where line-abrading obstructions like rocks aren't a factor.

Once hooked, muskies hooked on mono rarely get off. Finally, mono is definitely preferable to superlines for pulling in-line planer boards. Mono holds far better in a board's line releases, and the shock-absorbing ability helps keep fish hooked while reeling in and removing the board.

While most muskie anglers agree that superlines are the way to go, leaders are an area where there's far from universal agreement on what's best.

Many veteran anglers prefer single-strand wire leaders in the 100- to 170-pound-test range for most applications. Single-strand leaders are durable and fairly foolproof. Best of all, you can easily make them yourself by buying the wire, snaps, and swivels.

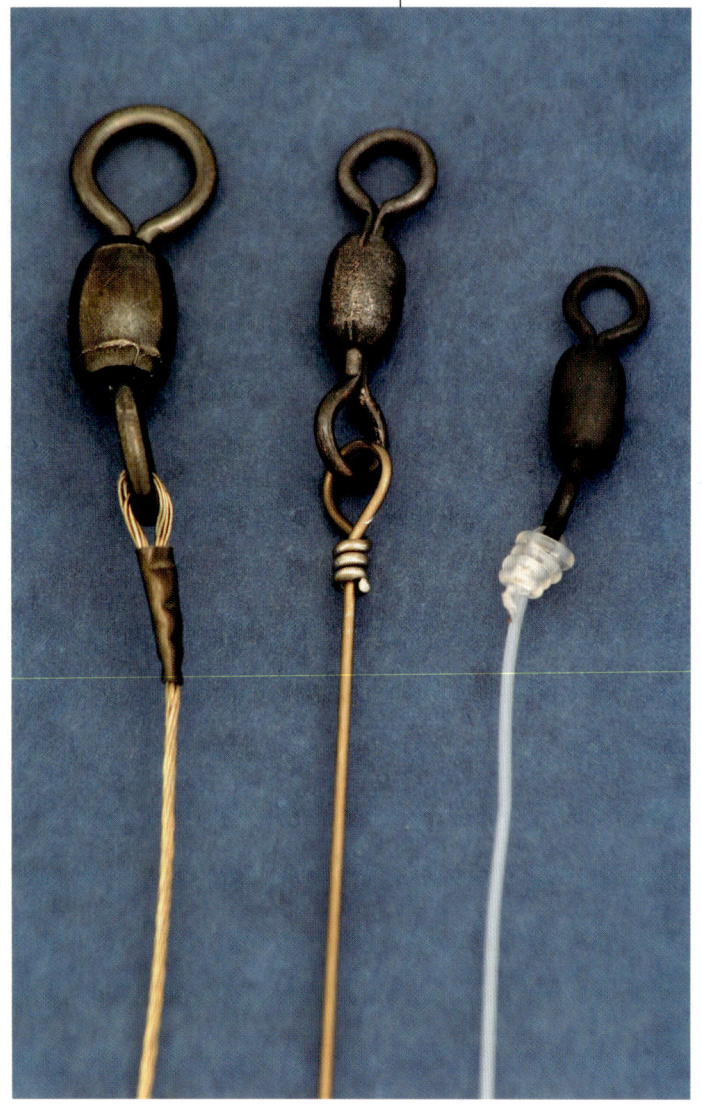

Leader options, left to right: stranded wire, single-strand wire, and fluorocarbon. DAVE OLSON

Stranded-wire leaders can also be used. These leaders require crimps, and some anglers distrust crimps as another potential failure point. While 7-strand leaders are the norm, for the past couple seasons we've been experimenting with 49-strand wire, which can be found in saltwater tackle catalogs. Forty-nine-strand wire seems softer and far less prone to kinking than 7-strand. Most important, it's far less abrasive, so it's much easier on fish that roll up in a long trolling leader—a common occurrence in cold water late in the fall.

Fluorocarbon leaders have become popular in the past few years. Fluorocarbon has nearly the same light refractive qualities as water, rendering the leader nearly invisible underwater. Whether leader visibility is a significant factor is highly debatable. You'd have a hard time convincing us a fish that's willing to eat a 9-inch, bright-orange block of wood would turn it down because it spotted a leader. Still, there's at least some credible anecdotal evidence that the low visibility of fluorocarbon can be an advantage on highly pressured waters. Fluorocarbon does have appeal for the same reasons as 49-strand wire, however. It's kink-free and very fish-friendly. It is not, however, very abrasion resistant and seems to lose strength quickly as soon as it becomes abraded. Use it with care around rocks, and if a fluoro leader shows signs of nicks or wear, replace it immediately. Using it for trolling around rocks is probably not a good idea at all. Fluoro is tough, but it can be still be cut. If you use fluorocarbon, break strengths of at least 100-pound test are definitely recommended. One hundred- to 130-pound test seems to be durable enough to withstand the abuse of muskie fishing without being so large in diameter it affects lure action.

How long should leaders be? For casting, 10- to 16-inch leaders are a balance between offering adequate protection for the line and being practical to use. Trolling leaders can be significantly longer—4 to 6 feet. Long trolling leaders protect the line when trolling around rocks and, as mentioned before, when fish roll in the line during the fight.

BOATS, MOTORS, AND OTHER OPTIONS

The essential components of a basic muskie fishing rig are a boat and an outboard motor, a bow-mount trolling motor, and a casting platform for one, two, or three anglers. The specifics, the specifications, for any particular angler's rig primarily depend on the waters he or she fishes.

Your waters may require a 16-foot aluminum boat with a 25- to 50-horsepower outboard. Or maybe a 21-foot fiberglass bass boat or multispecies (deep-V) boat powered by a 250-horsepower outboard suits you. Trolling motors range from 12-volt to 36-volt models. Twenty-four-volt models have become the standard on 17- to 20-foot boats.

Unconventional Alternatives to the Typical Muskie Rig

Do you fish a small pond, a stocked city lake, a wilderness hike-in lake? Do you want to get down in the water with the fish you are stalking? Then a pair of waders or a belly boat and kick fins will serve your purposes.

Kayaks and canoes are popular options for small rivers and hike-in lakes with no boat ramps.

Do you fish a lake where motor trolling is not allowed … and do you have energy to burn? Then a row trolling boat may be your ticket to a 50-incher.

Do you fish rivers with a lot of skinny water between muskie holes? Then a johnboat and a short-shaft 15-horse outboard is all you'll need.

Do you troll Lake St. Clair or Georgian Bay or the St. Lawrence River with four to six anglers in the boat? Then you may be running a 31-foot cruiser with twin inboards.

CHAPTER FOUR

Necessary Tools and Release Techniques

The size and power of muskies can lead to the impression that they're tough critters. The fact is, muskies are extremely fragile when mishandled. Especially the BIG ones. Yes, it's the biggest muskies that are most likely to succumb to mistreatment. With low population density and slow growth rates, a big fish that dies because it was handled poorly can take decades to replace. They're too rare and valuable a resource to mishandle. Especially now, with muskie fishing growing in popularity and pressure on the resource increasing, having a muskie fishery for the future makes successfully releasing fish today a necessity.

A lot of the tools that are necessary for responsible muskie fishing, catching, and releasing are intended to help you release a muskie as quickly and safely as possible. But that safety factor applies to your hide, too. The muskie's teeth are sharp, and the hooks you use are dangerous. Muskies are big, nasty critters. They can be difficult and dangerous to handle. Especially the BIG ones. A 35- or 40-pound muskie is shockingly powerful. We've both had trips cut short by unplanned visits to the emergency room when fishing partners got careless handling a big fish. The number of "must have" items for muskie fishing is pretty small. Release tools are certainly on that list of items. They're a "have them, or don't fish" necessity.

Your Muskie Tool Kit

Here's a list of tools you should have with you:

Long-nose pliers or hook-outs. Long hook-outs, whether they're needle-nose pliers or small-jawed, pistol-grip types such as those made by Baker, keep your hands away from teeth and hooks while you're unhooking a fish. Short, 8-inch models will work, but most muskie anglers prefer 11-inch models for more reach. A 30-pound muskie has a *big* mouth, with very big teeth, and reaching into one to remove a hook way down in it because your pliers are too short isn't fun. Pliers with a 45-degree angle to the jaws make seeing what you're doing a lot easier—the jaws aren't hidden behind your hand and forearm as you reach down into a fish's mouth, so we definitely recommend either them or long pliers with angled handles like those made by Snap-On.

Hook cutters. Powerful compound-pressure hook cutters—they're actually mini-bolt cutters—are used when hooks are too deeply embedded to be pulled out with more than a sharp tug. They're also a safety tool—should the worst happen and you become hooked to a fish, they're the fastest way to get free.

Quality matters with hook cutters. Cheap, bulk-bin cutters will only last for a few hooks before jaws begin to dull or spring off center, usually take two hands to cut large hooks, and can send cutoff hook points rocketing off at high velocity in random directions (including into your face or eyes). Some may not cut heavy, hardened hooks found on some muskie lures at all.

Required muskie release tools, left to right: 11-inch, 45-degree-angle needle-nose pliers, Knipex mini–bolt cutters, jaw spreaders.
DAVE OLSON

The best cutters we've found, bar none, are the mini-bolt cutters made by Knipex. Ours have lasted several seasons of frequent use. Cutting even 5/0 or 6/0 heavy hooks requires only a one-handed squeeze, and cut hook pieces simply fall off rather than flying at your head. Knipex cutters can be tough to find. Even large home improvement stores likely won't have them. Try good muskie tackle shops, or *The Next Bite—Esox Angler* magazine.

Jaw spreaders. Spring jaw spreaders are used to hold open the jaws of a fish so you can extract deeply embedded hooks. They're certainly not needed for every fish, but when you need them, you *really* need them. You can get by without jaw spreaders, but they're inexpensive, so bring them along.

Landing nets, cradles, and hybrid landing devices. The number-one function of a landing net is to corral the fish so that you can keep it in the water (and in the net) while you remove hooks. This takes a large net with a strong handle, a large hoop, and a large bag. A large, deep bag is a requirement for muskie nets. Too small a net will fold fish, and they'll fight the unnatural position. A large, wide bag allows fish to sit naturally in the water, and they'll be a lot calmer and easier to handle. Frabill and Beckman both make muskie-worthy nets. Both offer a coated, knotless mesh material, which is absolutely required to minimize damage to the fish. Knotted, uncoated bags will split fins and remove slime and scales, which can open the door to infection after the fish is released. It was not until coated knotless mesh became available that muskie nets began to see widespread use.

Along with traditional hoop and bag nets, there are other landing device options. Muskie cradles like the one available from Frabill are the ultimate in fish-friendly handling, as fish can rest naturally in the cradle while the hooks are removed. The drawback to cradles is they take some practice, and landing a fish with one is definitely a two-person operation. Finally, there is a hybrid device, the Frabill Kwik Kradle. Designed by our friend Pete Maina, it's a combination landing net and cradle with the hoop, bag, and handle of a traditional net, but with a scoop front and flat, long net bottom like a cradle. The Kwik Kradle is a very user- and fish-friendly landing device, with advantages of both traditional nets and cradles. They can take up a lot of room, which is a drawback in a smaller boat, but they're hard to beat in terms of ease of use and being good for the fish.

The authors team up to release a nice muskie. Landing devices like nets with large, deep bags allow you to keep fish contained while you unhook them. SARA KIMM

Release Techniques

Methods for releasing muskies can vary widely, depending on a number of factors: whether you have a landing device like a net or cradle available, how the fish is hooked, wind and water conditions (cold or very warm water), whether you plan to take photos (and what kind of photos you want), and, perhaps most of all, the experience of the angler. The fact is, any of the methods we'll be describing here can work if they're performed quickly, carefully, and competently. Or any of them can lead to an unsuccessful release if a few basic guidelines are ignored.

It's critical to remember that when releasing muskies, the factors that can cause stress and increase the possibility of delayed mortality are cumulative. Unusually warm water, too much time out of the water for photos or measurement, improper holds, or spending too much time trying to pull hooks out rather than cutting them—each of these factors

GOING BARBLESS

Perhaps the single biggest thing anglers can do to make release faster and more successful across the board is to pinch the barbs down on your hooks. With today's longer, softer rods, losing fish because of barbless hooks isn't much of an issue. After several seasons of using barbless hooks much of the time, neither of us has noticed any significant increase in lost fish. Weigh that against simple, fast unhooking, and barbless hooks are pretty appealing.

Barbless hooks are a safety factor for you as well. Suddenly finding yourself attached by a barbed 5/0 hook to a green, thrashing fish is an unforgettable experience, and not in a good way. You'll really appreciate barbless hooks if you do ever get stuck. If you fish at night, or fish alone a lot, going barbless is definitely recommended—for safety reasons alone.

alone is bad enough. But add them up, and there's an even greater increased risk of a fish being released, only to die later. Each additional factor increases that risk.

Whatever the conditions, time is the single biggest factor in making sure releases are successful. The quicker you can get a fish unhooked and back to where it came from, the better the chances are that fish will survive and thrive.

So have a plan. Have your release tools out and at hand before you begin fishing. If you plan to take photos, have the camera out and ready *before* the fish is at boatside.

Exactly how fish are unhooked depends on where the hooks are, and whether you're hand-landing or using a landing device.

Once it is at boatside, most anglers grab a fish using a hold known as a "lip lock." This hold immobilizes the fish's head so you can safely remove the hooks. To lip-lock a fish, curl your index and middle finger, then gently slide those two fingers under the gill cover and forward toward the fish's nose, applying slight outward pressure with your fingertips until your fingers stop just under the fish's jaw. Beneath the jaw, on the outside of the fish's mouth, there's a small notch between the throat and jawbone where your thumb should come to rest. If you've never done it before, practice on a mounted fish first if you can so that you can see where your fingers should and shouldn't go. Just don't stick your fingers straight into the gills. The gill filaments are extremely fragile, and the gill rakers are incredibly sharp.

Once the fish is under control, keep the fish's head in the water as much as possible. That's the part that breathes. Unhook the fish by popping hooks out with pliers. If a hook takes more than a firm tug to remove, cut the hooks. For fish in a net, we generally begin unhooking them by simply cutting every hook we can see. It's safer, faster, and easier when any loose-hanging hooks are out of the way. Hooks are cheap and easily replaced. Measure fish in the water with a floating ruler if you want a quick measurement.

Holds and Photos

For a lot of anglers, photos of fish are an important part of the experience. But holding fish for photos is definitely an added stress to caught fish, especially if the fish are held out of the water for any length of time. If you're going to get a photo, have the camera ready before the fish is ever picked up.

When you lift the fish, support its weight with one hand along the side of the fish or with its weight resting across a forearm. Support as much of the fish's weight as possible. Fish should only be out of the water for a few seconds—enough to snap a few quick shots. Ten to twenty seconds is all it should take.

If you take fish out of the water for a photo, support the fish's weight as much as possible. DAVE OLSON

If you're in a situation where additional stress-causing conditions like high water temperatures, heavy wind, and waves that make unhooking and handling the fish difficult are a factor, or if the fish just took a long time to unhook, skip the photo session altogether. If you want a photo, take an in-the-water release shot.

There's still some discussion in the muskie world about whether vertical holds are acceptable. To us the answer is a definitive no. Lifting a fish by the gills and holding it vertically puts incredible strain on the fish's muscular and skeletal structures, especially those around the head and gill arches. Damage to these vital areas can inhibit the fish's ability to breathe and feed after it's released. We've asked many fisheries biologists and fish physiologists about vertical holds, and all of them—*every single one*—has told us that vertical holds aren't an acceptable way of handling fish that are to be released. Don't take our word for it. Take theirs. Just don't do it.

Whatever methods you use to release fish, always keep in mind that time is of the essence. Get them unhooked and released as quickly as possible.

Other Necessary Tools and Equipment

Aside from release tools, there are a few more necessary items you should always have with you. Here's a short list:

First-aid kit: Adhesive bandages, gauze and tape, antiseptic wash—just for starters. The rest is up to you.

Lure repair kit: For replacing hooks that you cut during release, carry split ring pliers, spare hooks, and split rings. Carry a hook-sharpening file to sharpen these replacement hooks and to touch up hooks on lures that have been dulled by contact with rocks or muskies. Check and sharpen hooks *before* a muskie strikes. Don't wait till you lose one, like most people do.

CHAPTER FIVE

Follows, Figure Eights, and Triggering Fish

There are many reasons to enjoy fishing for and catching muskies. The way they fight can be spectacular. They're a mentally challenging and physically demanding species to pursue. They obviously get big.

But if you asked a handful of hard-core muskie anglers why they fish for muskies, it's a near certainty that the way muskies follow lures to the boat and strike them at boatside will come up several times. In fact, it'll probably be the first thing many of them mention.

Other fish follow lures, certainly. Smallmouth bass do it in bunches, and pike follow lures frequently. Even walleyes, more often than you think. But none do it with the same frequency, the same aggression, or the same attitude that muskies do. And none are as willing to strike lures at the side of the boat on a figure eight with an angler standing over the top of them.

Learning how to react to following muskies, performing figure eights well, and triggering fish in general is a major part of becoming more successful as a muskie angler. At sport shows and seminars, we talk to lots of anglers who may catch one or two fish a year on a figure eight. For these anglers, it's a rare and noteworthy event. On the other hand, some of the best muskie anglers we know may catch nearly half their fish each season at boatside.

Why the disparity? These successful anglers have mastered their approach when reacting to following fish—from spotting them, to attempting to trigger them, to figure eights. These are skills that are critical to becoming a more successful muskie angler. Many of the details of muskie techniques can be mentioned in passing as we describe seasonal patterns and tactics later on, but in our book (and this *is* our book), figure eights and triggering techniques deserve their own chapter. They're that important.

The First Step: Seeing Follows

If you look at muskie fishing magazines and Internet message boards, there's usually a lot of discussion about strategies and tactics for getting following fish to bite, but much of the time an important detail—in some ways *the* most important—is ignored: actually seeing the things.

Simply put, the earlier in the retrieve you can spot following fish, and the farther away from the boat you can begin manipulating your lure to either trigger them or change their mood, the better your chances of catching the fish. At the very least, spotting fish away from the boat gives you a chance to get over your initial excitement and get your act together so you can do a decent figure eight. If you only spot fish when your retrieve is finished and you're already thinking about your next cast, your odds of converting the follow into a strike are pretty low.

The first step in spotting more fish and seeing them farther away from the boat is getting a good pair of polarized sunglasses. Polarized glasses cut surface glare and allow you to see into the water. As a piece of equipment, they are arguably more important than any other single piece of equipment. Depth finder is broken? Oh, well. I'll get by, and get it fixed when I get home. Forgot my sunglasses in the truck? Turn the boat around. They're that important.

Which glasses to get will likely depend on your budget. Polarized sunglasses can range in price from a few dollars to a couple hundred dollars. There's no doubt, though, that you get what you pay for, with glass lenses being far superior to plastic or polycarbonate lenses. Quality sunglasses are also far better when it comes to protecting your eyes from damage to long-term UV exposure. We've found Ocean Waves in the Backwater Green lens color to be excellent for spotting fish under most conditions, but Orvis, Maui Jim, and Costa Del Mar are all good options, too. Whatever brand you choose, get the best you can afford. If it comes down to a choice between a few new lures or a better pair of sunglasses, get the glasses. You'll catch more fish.

Once you've got some quality glasses, the next piece of the puzzle is learning to spot following fish. In all truthfulness, getting better at seeing fish, like so many things in muskie fishing, is mainly a function of time on the water and training yourself to look for the sometimes subtle clues that you have a fish behind your lure. But there are some things you can do to speed up the process.

Most important, certainly, is being aware of *where* you're looking as you search for follows. All too often, anglers will focus on the lure itself, rather

Learning a few basic triggering techniques is often the difference between a follow and a fish in the net. SARA KIMM

than behind the lure where the fish are going to be. It's understandable, sort of. Muskie lures are neat, and you do need to pay attention to how your lures are working and what you're fishing them through. Besides, there's often not much else to look at. But you need to force yourself to only glance at the lure occasionally and focus on an area behind the lure from, say, 1 to 6 feet behind it, and slightly below it.

What do you look for? Anything. Rarely will you see the whole fish at first, especially in darker water or windy conditions, or far away from the boat. Most often you'll simply see something that doesn't look quite right—the water behind the lure will just change color suddenly. You'll see a flash of white from the underside of a fish's jaw or inside its mouth, a moving fin, or weeds pushed out of the way as a fish passes through them. With topwaters, small swirls or ripples a few feet behind the bait can give a following fish away. Sometimes it's just a shadow, or the perception of movement. Often—and this sounds odd, but it's true—it's just a feeling that something isn't right. Your brain spots something different or out of place long before you consciously recognize what you're seeing as a fish. Good anglers react instantly to those instincts, and begin trying to get the fish to hit.

Triggering Following Fish

So how do you trigger a fish that's following your lure into striking?

Consider what's happening out there in the water. You've managed to attract a fish's interest enough to get it to spend the energy to move, and follow your lure. Your job now is to continue to keep changing the fish's mood until it's aggressive enough to strike.

Techniques for triggering following fish generally boil down to some combination of two factors: speed and erratic action. What you're able to do to trigger a fish can depend largely on what type of lure you're using. Some lure styles, with a wide speed range and wide tolerance for erratic action, give you lots of options. Others, with a more narrow range of capabilities, make your job a lot harder because of their limited speed range or limited tolerance for being worked erratically without rolling over, spinning out of control, or just flat out not working right.

We'll begin the discussion with bucktails and spinnerbaits, since they're probably the easiest lures to learn to trigger following fish with. Often enough with bucktails, simple speed is all it takes. When you spot a following fish, immediately begin to gradually speed up your retrieve. Speed it up how much? Let the fish's reaction tell you. Start with an initial burst of speed. If the fish responds immediately by accelerating to catch up, keep increasing the speed as long as the fish will do the same. If the fish *doesn't* react to a first burst of speed, or reacts slowly, reel at a steady pace until the fish catches up, then add a short burst of speed once again, or change the bucktail's pace and action by steadily and gently twitching the rod tip downward, making the skirt and blade pulse, then gradually speed up again to see if the change in action has changed the fish's mood enough to get it to accelerate.

The goal of increasing speed with bucktails is to turn the fish's pursuit of your lure into a game of keep-away. Convince the fish that it's chasing fleeing prey. Playing keep-away is counterintuitive, especially to beginning muskie anglers. After all, you *want* them to catch up to your lure and eat it. But keep this in mind: For short bursts, muskies can swim up to 30-plus miles per hour. Play keep-away. If they want to win, they will.

If you've gradually increased your speed without triggering the fish, adding a direction change is the next step. As the bucktail nears the boat, say 20 to 30 feet away, begin changing direction by swinging your rod tip slowly from side to side, making the bucktail swing from side to side in curves that gradually grow wider as the lure nears the boat.

Triggering fish with jerkbaits and crankbaits can be more difficult. They usually lack the speed range bucktails and spinnerbaits have, so retrieve speed can only be increased to the point where the lure begins to go out of control. The bigger problem, though, is that many of these lures, jerkbaits especially, are already moving erratically, and if that erratic action wasn't enough to trigger a fish right off the bat, it can be difficult to make them more so and keep the lure working properly.

Your best shot with jerkbaits is to change the frequency or beat of the bait's action. If you are working a diver jerkbait like a Suick through a weedbed with long, slow pulls and a muskie shows itself, pick up the pace. Switch over to 6-inch jerks—chop, chop, chop. Make that Suick look like a baitfish suddenly reacting to the muskie and fleeing in panic. It's a little trickier with gliders, because the beat of the retrieve is so critical to maintaining the right action. Here's where it's important to know your bait,

THE IMPORTANCE OF DIRECTION CHANGES

Regardless of lure type, one of the simplest and most effective triggering techniques for following fish is a simple direction change. The figure eight itself is nothing more than a series of constant direction changes that can trigger a fish into striking. But there's no reason to wait until a fish gets to boatside to begin using direction changes to trigger them.

Imagine a straight line drawn from your rod tip, through your lure and the following fish. With a perfectly straight retrieve, the line of travel for lure and fish won't change much at all. Who knows why, but the sooner you can begin getting a following fish to break out of a straight line of travel and start moving in response to the bait, either horizontally or vertically, the more likely it is to hit. If you can get a fish turning its head from side to side or, better yet, "snaking" its entire body behind a lure, your odds of catching the fish soar.

Change a lure's direction by steadily sweeping the rod tip from side to side as you continue your retrieve. Start the direction change 30 feet or so from the boat. As the lure gets closer, the change in angle from rod tip to lure increases, taking the lure in ever-wider S-turns, gradually bringing the fish farther and farther out of a straight line of travel. A series of S-turns, then a sudden direction change right at boatside as you begin a figure eight can be a deadly combination for following fish.

Horizontal direction changes can work with virtually any lure. With some, like topwaters, they're about your only option. With some lure types, though, especially bucktails and spinnerbaits, vertical direction changes are possible as well. When a fish is spotted following a bucktail, along with an increase in speed, try slowly lifting your rod tip to lift the bait higher in the water column. Many muskies hit just as the bucktail's blade begins to bulge the surface. If the fish continues to follow, drop your rod back down as the bait nears the boat, and begin to S-turn. A great thing about a vertical direction change is it can be accomplished much farther from the boat than horizontal S-turns. Beginning with a vertical change in direction, then adding S-turns and finally a boatside L-turn, is a tremendously effective combination of triggers. For some reason, though, few anglers consider vertical changes in direction as a means of triggering strikes.

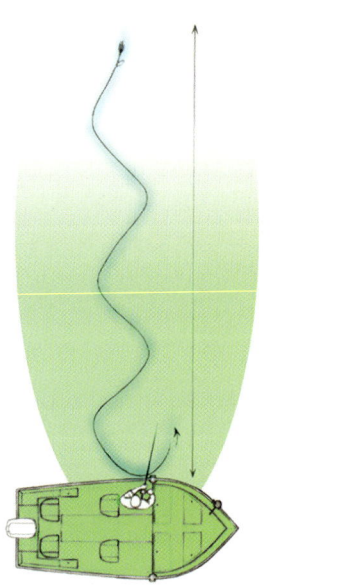

to know its range. When a muskie follows a glider, try taking the glider up toward its upper limit in speed and rhythm. Or sometimes holding the beat, but slowing down on the reel speed will make the lure dance in place. For both divers and gliders, on the figure eight, drive the bait deep on the straightaways, maintaining the high-frequency panic moves, and bring it back toward the surface on the turns.

Crankbaits give you a few more options than jerkbaits. They usually have a somewhat wider speed range than most jerkbaits, so along with increasing the action with twitches and pauses, you can gradually increase lure speed. One of the simplest and most effective techniques for crankbaits, especially deep-diving baits like Triple-Ds or flat-sided baits like Shallow Invaders or Jakes, is a brief pause with a very slight (a few inches) dip of the rod tip to give the line a little slack, then a short, sharp, upward snap of the wrist. Not a heaving rip—just a sharp snap that lifts the rod tip about a foot. The bait will hang briefly on the pause, then dart suddenly off to one side or the other.

Tactics for triggering fish with topwaters can vary widely depending on lure type. Tail-spinning baits or propbaits can be sped up similar to bucktails, at least to the point where they begin to roll over. Walk-the-dog topwaters can be sped up somewhat, but a preferred tactic by many hard-core walk-the-dog fans is to maintain the pace and intensity of taps of the rod, but slow down the reel speed, slightly feeding the bait slack on each twitch. With more slack, walk-the-dog baits will dart farther out to the side while slowing their forward motion slightly. Done carefully, and with a little practice, the lure can almost appear to walk in place. It's a tremendous trigger with these types of lures.

Slower moving topwaters like creepers or wobblers are much tougher. Often speed simply isn't an option. Even twitches can sometimes cause these lures to blow out of the water. Increase your speed as much as the lure will allow, then change direction by sweeping your rod from side to side as the lure gets closer. Sometimes bringing the lure to a dead stop can cause fish to hit, either during a long pause or as the lure begins moving again. But this is usually an all-or-nothing proposition. Fish either hit it or leave. Often enough, the only thing you can do with lures of this type is hope the fish hits it before it gets to the boat.

KNOW YOUR TOOLS

Triggering following fish, whether during the cast or at boatside on a figure eight, relies on being able to do more with the lure the fish is following. Successful figure eights rely on steadily increasing speed and being able to maneuver lures around corners without them spinning out, rolling on their sides, or otherwise quitting whatever action it was that attracted a fish in the first place. Triggering fish away from the boat requires additional erratic action, more speed, or both.

Each lure, with the possible exception of bucktails, has a range of what it can handle in terms of how fast it can be retrieved or how aggressively it can be worked. To successfully manipulate them to trigger a following fish, you have to be aware of what those limits are. Leave yourself some room, so to speak, in the lure's range of capabilities to attempt some of the triggering techniques we describe. It's especially important when it comes to figure eights. Bucktails can handle virtually any speed, but most crankbaits and jerkbaits can only go so fast before going totally out of control. Corners complicate things

further. Some lures simply don't turn corners too well. They may move fairly fast in a straight line but immediately roll over or blow out on corners, even at moderate speed.

Going into the first turn of a figure eight with a 25-pounder right behind the lure is not the time to discover how well your lures do in a figure eight. Get to know what your lures can handle, and come up with an alternative (slowing down on corners and accelerating on straightaways for lures that don't corner well, or walking lures around the boat rather than doing a figure eight) for lures with limitations on what they can handle. When we get new lures, one of the first things we do is find out what its quirks are in terms of speed and how it can be worked without going out of control. Run it through a figure eight. See how it corners. What happens when you twitch it hard, or give it a burst of speed? Find out before there's a fish behind it. Many a golden opportunity for boatside mayhem has been blown because this simple step was skipped.

Boatside Tactics: L-turns and the Figure Eight

Boatside strikes on a figure eight are one of the most thrilling moments in muskie fishing. Properly executing a figure eight is also one of the most technically demanding aspects of the sport. Though the fundamentals of the technique are simple, learning them, and smoothly putting them into practice (rather than going suddenly and thoroughly to pieces) when there's a big muskie bearing down on you, isn't simple at all. Becoming competent takes hours of practice. Becoming an expert can take years.

Effective boatside maneuvers begin with being ready, with good rod and body position. By the end of your retrieve, your rod tip should be pointing nearly directly downward at the six o'clock position, with the rod tip just above or slightly in the water. Ideally you should be standing with your feet underneath you and stable, with your shoulders square to the following fish. Standing upright and stable isn't always easy if you're running a bow-mount trolling motor, especially in big wind and waves, but it's impossible if you're sitting slouched down in a boat seat. Lurching to your feet so that you can figure-eight when you spot a following fish close to the boat will almost invariably spook the fish when it spots sudden movement from above. Throughout the entire process at boatside, keep movement above the water to the absolute minimum, especially in clear water.

With your lure nearing boatside, the first step in the figure eight is a sudden change in direction—the L-turn. Retrieve until the end of your leader is within 2–3 inches of your rod tip. Now, with the hand you turn the reel handle with, quickly free spool the reel, and clamp your thumb down tightly on the spool. In the same motion, sweep the lure in a right angle along the side of the boat, making an L with the rod tip. Especially with fast-moving lures and aggressive fish, the L-turn alone will often trigger a strike.

So why free spool the reel? Most muskie anglers, us included, have their drag set fairly tight when casting to prevent the drag from slipping on a hookset. At boatside, a tight drag and a hooked muskie on less than a foot of line is a recipe for disaster. Going toe to toe with a just-hooked, thrashing muskie will almost invariably lead to the hooks pulling out and the fish getting off. In the worst case scenario, the line, snap, or leader will fail, and the fish will swim off with a lure in its mouth, only to die later. Even on the off chance the fish stays hooked, backing off on the drag can

Figure eights begin with an L-turn at the boat. You should make an L-turn after every cast.
SARA KIMM

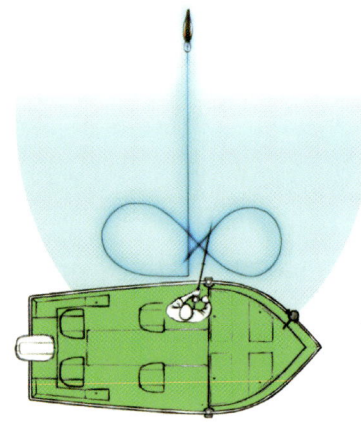

be difficult when trying to fight a fish, especially a big one. Hitting free spool after the fact can be impossible when there's too much tension on the spool to push the button. Frantically pounding on the free spool button with the heel of your hand while you chase a big fish that's barreling down the side of the boat is exciting, but not something you want to make a habit of. A friend of ours was once actually *pulled out of the boat* by a very large muskie that hit at boatside, then decided to be somewhere else before he could release the spool tension.

If a fish doesn't hit on the L-turn, it's time to figure-eight. From the end of the L-turn, sweep your rod tip out from the edge of the boat into a wide turn, then angle back toward the gunwale and around into another turn.

At its most basic, a figure eight should be a smoothly executed maneuver. It's critical that turns be as wide and smooth as possible. Muskies, especially big ones, don't corner too well (think semitrailer rather than sports car), and if they can't track the lure through the turns, they'll quickly lose interest and swim off. Long rods obviously help with wide turns, and so does being

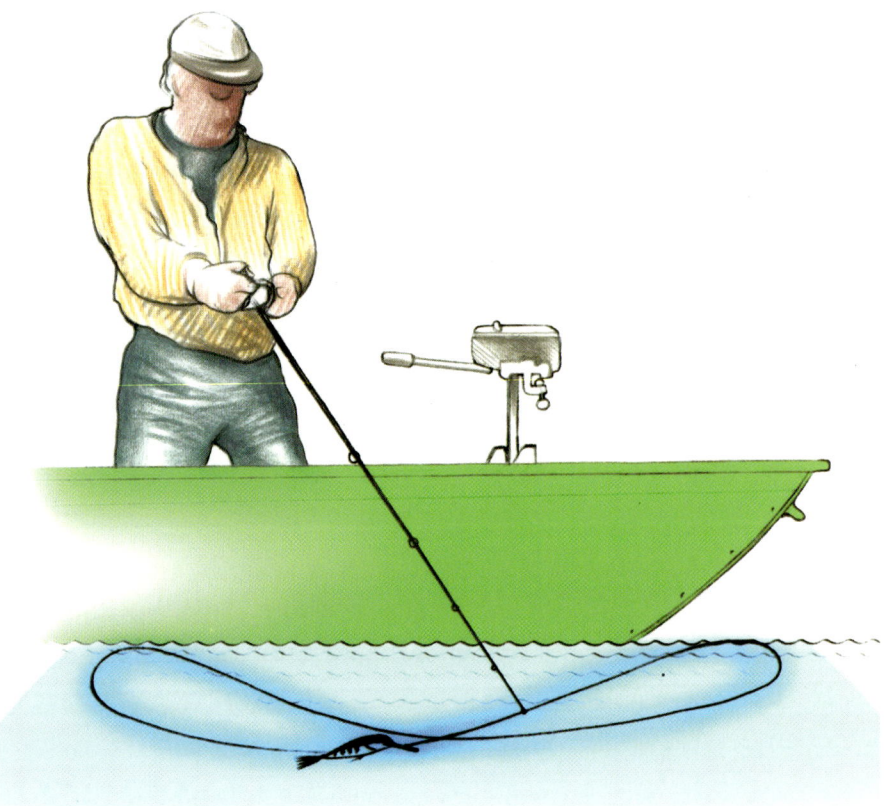

aware of how far you can reach. Ideally, the very outside end of each turn should be just about to the end of your reach.

A lot of anglers will sometimes make a large oval rather than an actual "8." Ovals can work better with lures that don't corner very well, with fast-moving lures, or with big fish. We both will choose an oval over an "8" for large fish because it's a little easier for a big fish to track a speeding lure through an oval. Especially when you're learning, an oval can be less complicated and just as effective most of the time.

As the fish follows the lure through the figure eight or oval, gradually speed up the lure, and concentrate on playing keep-away with the fish. Not slowing down but deliberately trying to keep the bait away from the fish is difficult to force yourself to do at first. *Not* allowing the fish to catch the bait goes against your every instinct. Unless you're using an extremely fast lure like a burned bucktail, though, slowing down is almost always a mistake until the fish is actually trying to grab the lure. Slow down, and fish most often lose interest.

Much of the success good figure-eight artists have with triggering fish at boatside comes from their ability to not only smoothly execute the basic mechanics but also to gauge the fish's mood and willingness to chase the lure, and respond accordingly. Watching the fish's behavior, and looking for "body language" like snapping jaws, rapid head movements or snaking, twitching bodies, is something that can only be learned through experience and time on the water.

When fish show aggression by nipping or snapping, or simply continue to follow but refuse to commit, there are a few more tricks you can try. A simple but effective one is driving the bait downward on a straight-away, then bringing the lure up over the fish's head on corners—a three-dimensional approach to figure eights.

For how long should you figure-eight? As long as the fish stays around, keep at it. If the fish leaves, note its attitude. Did the fish seem very aggressive but then suddenly race off, almost as if it were spooked? Keep with the figure eight. Sometimes it seems as though hot fish will circle wide on the bait and line up for a rush at it. They can disappear, only to roar in out of nowhere to eat the bait. If the fish just slowly swims off or, worse yet, simply sinks straight down, it's perhaps a neutral or negative fish that you might need to return to later.

And if the fish hits? It's tempting to simply lift straight upward. Don't.

WHY WE DON'T FIGURE-EIGHT AFTER EVERY CAST

There's a school of thought that advises performing a complete figure eight after every cast. The reasoning, more or less, is so you have a chance to catch "those fish you never see coming."

Neither of us figure-eights after every cast. Nor do most of the best anglers we know. To us, it's about efficiency. A full figure eight takes time. It's also tiring. If there isn't a fish visible and following, you're better off making another cast and getting the lure back out to where the fish are than you are flailing around beside the boat for an invisible fish that is probably not there at all.

We do, after every cast, perform an L-turn at boatside. An L-turn gives you an extra few seconds to scan for a late-appearing fish (and also usually turns those fish so you can spot their sides). It lets you turn smoothly into a figure eight if you do spot a fish, or quickly pick up the lure and make

another cast if you don't. The only situations where we'd do a full figure eight after each cast is after dark, in extremely heavy algae blooms, or other situations where you simply can't see into the water at all.

Our friend and legendary Lake of the Woods guide Doug Johnson probably summed up the argument against every-cast figure eights best: "It's like deer hunting," said Johnson. "You don't just start shooting into the woods. You usually wait until you see a deer first."

Advocates of the every-cast figure eight will tell you it boats them an extra fish or two a season. Maybe. But we'd argue that if you don't spend time and effort figure-eighting a fish that overwhelming probability says isn't there, and make another cast to where they live, you'll boat far more than one or two.

Concentrate on setting the hook back into the fish, parallel to the fish's body and opposite the direction the fish was moving. If a fish hits on the turn, at the end of your reach, sometimes the best option is to simply drive the rod tip downward and back against the fish as best you can. Setting straight upward drives hooks up to the hard, bony roof of the fish's mouth, and hooking percentages are pretty low. Setting the hook back into the fish will (usually) put the hooks in the corner of the fish's mouth.

When the fish is hooked, play the fish by thumbing the spool until the fish swims away from the boat. Some fish, often big ones, simply won't make a run but will instead sit beside the boat with their head out of the water, trying to shake the lure loose. As often as not, they do just that. Aside from saying, "Oh, no!" and hoping for the best, about all you can do is try to move the fish back into the water by driving your rod tip into the water.

The Final Word on Triggering Fish

The techniques for triggering following fish are learned skills, and they take practice. Putting the whole sequence together when there's a 35-pounder with her nose in the tail of your lure isn't always easy, especially at first. If you're new to muskies, expect to botch a few opportunities as you learn what works best for you. Much of the process relies on instincts and reflexes, which take time to practice and develop. So practice.

But here's the part of the picture too many muskie anglers miss. You don't have to wait until you see a fish to try triggering them. Wind, water color, glare—all can keep you from spotting following fish until they're right at your feet. Most of the techniques we've described for triggering fish away from the boat can—and should—be done on each retrieve, at least briefly. As a rule of thumb, never just cast and reel. Pause crankbaits and jerkbaits, or twitch them sharply a time or two at some point in every cast. Vary your speed with topwaters, and S-turn at the end of each retrieve. Gradually speed up bucktails or spinnerbaits throughout the retrieve on every cast, or simply double your retrieve speed for a few cranks in the middle of the retrieve. Following fish often overtake a bucktail with a burst of speed as soon as it begins to surge away from them. A great triggering technique for bucktails and spinnerbaits is to vary your speed on each crank of the reel handle. Think of the path of the reel handle as a clock face. From the twelve to six o'clock position, crank about half again as fast as you do from the six to twelve o'clock position. It takes no more effort than a straight retrieve but makes a bucktail pulse steadily in the water. It's a simple technique, and a great triggering tool.

Once you have the fundamental mechanics down to the point where you don't have to think about them anymore, you can concentrate on what the fish is doing and how it's responding. Eventually, reacting to following fish with something more helpful than "There's one!" will become second nature. Get to that point, and your catch rates at boatside will definitely begin to climb.

This early-season muskie bit on a figure eight. Practice boatside maneuvers so that you're ready when a fish like this follows your lure. MARK JOHNSON

CHAPTER SIX

Postspawn to Early Summer
(May into late June in the northern tier)

The theme of the postspawn spring period is the muskie's recovery from the rigors of spawning and a gradual transition into aggressive feeding as the waters warm.

Note: This period is often the time of the muskie season opener. In many states and provinces, the season is closed earlier in the spring to protect spawners. But even where the regulations do not protect spawning muskies, we hope you do so voluntarily.

On most lakes, muskies spawn in shallow weedy bays when water temperatures are in the high 40s to low 50s. Female muskies usually deposit their eggs in just a few feet of water. But on some larger lakes, such as Leech Lake in northern Minnesota, tracking studies have shown that spawning can take place on deeper open-water flats in very large bays. This is an evolved survival tactic on lakes where there is a significant spawning pike population in the shallow bays.

In regions with no closed season, or in late-spring years where cold conditions push spawning into the open season, fishing is generally poor. Fish that are caught tend to be the smaller males.

Muskie spawning is a violent affair, often leaving muskies with open wounds and split fins. Female muskies tend to abandon spawning areas fairly quickly after depositing their eggs, but they usually don't go far right away. They need to rest and recover. For the larger females, recovery—and the transition back to a feeding mode—often takes a week or more, making postspawn a tough time for finding and catching larger fish.

Smaller male muskies, though, often hang around spawning areas during the postspawn period and are comparatively easier to catch.

Things start to improve as we get further away from the spawn itself. Females gradually recover from their postspawn period of inactivity. Three positive factors come together: one biological, one environmental, and one circumstantial. These muskies are hungry. They haven't eaten much in a while, and need to restore depleted energy reserves expended during the rigors of spawning. This need to gain energy comes at a time when warming water is starting to speed up their metabolism, further increasing energy demands. Best of all, these factors converge at a time when fish are relatively uneducated after a winter of little or no fishing pressure. Good times are just around the corner.

This theme of transition also applies to the muskie's environment. In addition to rising water temperatures, spring is a time of developing weed growth. Weed growth attracts baitfish and provides ambush cover for the muskies. This is where the transition period tips in our favor.

Finding Postspawn Muskies: The Big Bang Theory

One way to look at the location of muskies during this early-season transition period is to compare it to the big bang theory of the creation of the universe. (Bear with us for a minute.) That theory posits that the universe started with a small, infinitely dense core of matter exploding with a big … well … bang. In milliseconds, the universe expanded quite rapidly. It is evidently still expanding to this day. The point here is that matter flew out from a central point and dispersed outward from there.

This is where we get back to muskies. In early spring, spawning locations (shallow, weedy bays on waters with Wisconsin-strain muskies or middepth flats where Leech Lake strain fish spawn) are the core—dense concentrations of muskie matter. Postspawn, the transition involves dispersal of the matter (muskies) out away from the core (spawning areas). How rapidly that dispersal from areas of concentration occurs correlates not to time but directly to the progression of environmental conditions, such as water temperature, weed development, and the presence of forage species, from ice-out to early summer.

Tactical Factors

When the season starts—when you fish muskies for the first time in the spring—an awareness of where muskies are at in the postspawn transition is essential. Are they still spawning? Are they recovering? How long have they had to recover? Are they already starting to look for food? Are they aggressive or lethargic?

Rocky points outside spawning bays can be key early-season muskie spots on Canadian Shield waters. MARY COLSON-BURNS

Often, it's impossible to answer these questions right off the bat. You don't have days or weeks of time on the water chasing muskies to inform you. So how do you go about answering those questions?

Basic questions about the muskie's environment provide clues. Is it an early or late spring? How long ago did the ice go out? When did the spawn occur? (Ask bass or panfish anglers if they've seen muskies in the shallows.) What is the water temperature? What, generally, has the weather been like lately? Sunny and warm? Cold and cloudy? Has the water temperature risen rapidly recently, or has there been a slow, gradual warming?

Answers to these questions determine where to look for muskies—and also how to catch them. Let's look at some examples.

A Late (Cold) Spring

Let's say that the ice went out later than normal, the water didn't warm particularly fast, and the weeds haven't come up much. Let's say that the water temperature is only 59 degrees.

What would we expect to find? Our guess would be that the muskies have spawned fairly recently. Small, catchable male muskies will likely be lingering in or near spawning areas, while female muskies would be hunkered down in adjacent areas—nearby, but lethargic and recovering.

With poor weed development, male muskies often relate to hard cover such as stumps, timber, docks, and boulders, or they may move into extremely shallow water over sand or mud bottoms simply because it's the warmest water around.

Female muskies, without a deep weedline to hide in, would be near the first available cover just outside spawning areas. Typical spots would be breaklines, points, rock reefs, deep inside turns, and channels. Some may simply suspend at middle depths off the nearest breakline.

For fishing cooler water with minimum vegetation, we may want to use presentations that are slow and subtle. Water is often at its clearest in spring, so shallow muskies can spook easily. Smaller lures that don't make a big splash may work best.

An Early (Warm) Spring

Let's say that the ice went out earlier than normal, the water warmed up fast, and the weeds are thick and green. Let's say that the water temperature is in the mid-high 60s.

What would we expect to find? We would be pretty sure that, unless there's been an extremely intense hot spell, the spawn occurred weeks ago. Larger muskies should be fully recovered, hungry, and aggressive. With healthy weeds in bays or on the flats, feeding muskies could be up on the flats, cruising the weed edges, or already using points, reefs, and other midlake structure.

The best spots often combine two or three elements. A thick weed patch in a bay full of gravel and rocks, a few large boulders in a weedy bay, the intersection of a stump line with a weedbed—these are all potential muskie magnets. The presence of baitfish will usually determine which types of spots hold muskies.

With thick vegetation and cover, and in warmer water, muskies are usually not as spooky. Larger traditional muskie lures work just fine.

A Mixed-up Spring
(Early ice-out, warm for a few weeks, then cold)
As nice as it is when it happens, spring is seldom a steady progression of gradually warming water. Often enough, a late-spring cold snap can throw the brakes on everything. Suppose that the ice went out earlier than normal, the water warmed up quickly at first, but then a cold, cloudy, rainy weather pattern took over. The water stopped getting warmer, and the temperature even dropped a little. Weed growth has more or less stalled. The water temperature is in the high 50s. This weather pattern is more common than you might think.

What would we expect to find? With that early ice-out date, and an early warm period, muskies may well have spawned weeks ago. But the recent period of cold, cloudy weather has really slowed down the normal progression from postspawn to presummer patterns. Cool but stable, or cool and declining water temperatures are an important indicator of a fishery in neutral. Muskies have probably recovered from spawning, and large females have dispersed from their spawning areas. But with the low temperatures, the fish have probably not advanced to a true, early-summer, heavy feeding mode. Larger fish may even be somewhat lethargic. With little weed growth to attract baitfish and concentrate muskies, fish can be scattered across a range of potential locations; a few fish still lingering in spawning areas, a few more on nearby rock or other hard-bottomed areas like sand or gravel points or shorelines, even some suspended off the breakline over confined areas of open water. What's more, fish activity could probably be described as neutral at best. Fish may move up onto shallow flats on warm, sunny afternoons and warm evenings and become somewhat more active, but overall activity is low. With a range of potential locations, none of them holding particularly active fish, unstable or cooling weather in spring can make finding and catching muskies a real challenge.

Given the variety of location possibilities and generally low activity level, everything from small jigs to large trolling lures can work at this time, depending on the kinds of spots you're covering at the moment.

A BIT ON OLIGOTROPHIC LAKES

Because oligotrophic lakes are deeper and colder, tend to have a later ice-out date, and have few weeds even at their peak, the timing of every stage in the muskie's spring transition is later. All the same factors and needs are there. They just happen later. That could be good or bad.

Many experienced muskie anglers choose to open their season on oligotrophic lakes, because they know that the muskies will still be shallow and near their spawning bays. Until they come back just before ice-up in the late fall, this is often the best chance of the year to contact monster muskies on these waters. With the clear, cold water of spring and very little weed growth, subtle presentations are often the only way to go.

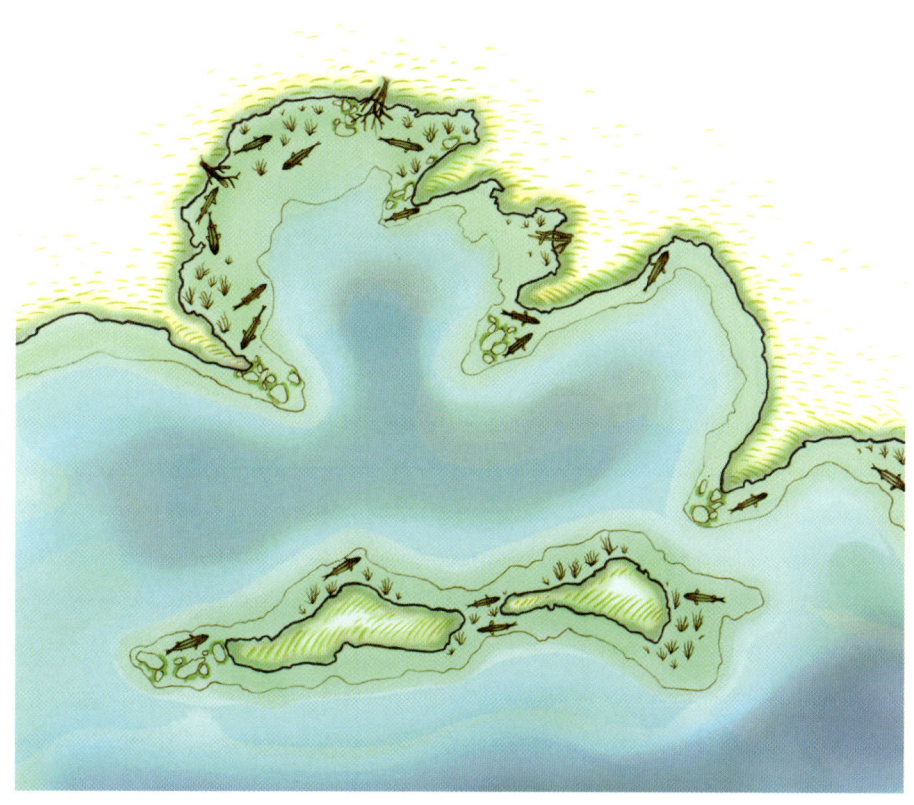

Tactics and Techniques

After you consider the local conditions and make an educated guess about which stage of the transition your lake is in, the next step is to go out and discover what is actually happening—find what you're looking for.

Under good to great conditions, fully recovered, feeding muskies will be on classic summer spots. They will be hungry, still uneducated, and aggressive. Under poor conditions—a late, cold spring or after a spring cold snap—smaller males will be easier to fool, but the big fish you're looking for may be a little trickier.

Whatever the spring has been like, the logical place to start is near likely spawning areas. Think back to the big bang theory. Spawning areas are the last known location of most of the muskies in the system. Why not start there?

On mesotrophic Canadian Shield lakes, like Lake of the Woods, this means looking in and just outside shallow, weedy spawning bays. If the water is warm and there are deep, lush weeds out on the edge, there could be some big muskies on that edge. Most likely, it won't be quite that easy. Look for routes out of spawning areas—at the first points of contact for fish traveling from the spawning areas to their summer spots. The points that mark the edges of the bay, the deep drop-off outside the bay, the nearby reefs, saddles, humps, and islands. But you may also want to go back into the backs of bays—especially if there are weed/rock or weed/stump combinations.

On lakes with Leech Lake–strain muskies that spawn over deeper water, spawning areas can be a little tougher to identify with certainty, but large shallow flats are a good starting point. From there, the process is similar: Seek out likely travel routes to summer areas, and then focus on pivot points along that route—like points, inside weedlines, inside turns along nearby breaklines, or shallow newly developed weedbeds.

Early in any muskie fishing outing—the first few hours of a day on the water or the first day of

The postspawn period has a reputation for being tough. But muskies haven't been pressured, and big fish like this one are more likely to make a mistake.
DAVE PAPERMASTER

a seven-day fishing trip—your goal is to find the fish. After asking all the right questions about the environmental variables and making an educated guess about where the muskies are in their transition, the good part kicks in: the finding.

Searching Efficiently—Pattern Sampling

During times of transition like the post-spawn period, muskies are usually much harder to "pattern" than more abundant fish, like bass. Many experts laugh at the idea of even trying to pattern muskies. And others think that muskies are relatively easy to pattern. Let's define "patterning" as an attempt to learn muskie activity level and the types of habitat that are holding muskies at a given point in the season. The only way to learn where the muskies are and what they are doing is on the water.

Pattern sampling refers to trying out all the different *types* of habitat that could be holding muskies. But it's *not* simply just going and fishing everything in sight. It's a fairly quick but deliberately thought-out survey of potential areas, based on where you think muskies are in their transition from postspawn to summer, and keeping in mind likely travel routes and local conditions. Given all these possibilities, it's important to make your best guess about where to start and then fish fairly quickly until you establish—OK, not a pattern—but at least a more educated guess on location/habitat/structure types that put you in contact with muskies.

Fish the outside edges of spawning bays and first points. If you find healthy weeds and warm water, work the weeds thoroughly. If the weedbeds and edges produce small muskies, you should move out to nearby reefs, channel edges, saddles, and points. If the deeper adjacent structures don't produce, you should keep moving out toward midlake structures. But before you venture too far out to sea, make sure you check out the backs of bays. These backwater spots can hold big muskies, especially if there is an inside weedline or intersecting structure such as boulders, stumps, or bulrushes.

If you start at the outside edges of spawning bays and adjacent points, but find little weed growth in the bays, then you should leave the bays and turn to the nearby spots that offer good ambush edges.

A BIT ABOUT OPEN WATER

While many muskies remain in relatively shallow water as they transition from postspawn to summer locations, in many lakes at least some muskies—and sometimes lots of them—seem to skip the whole business and simply hightail it to nearby open water. Radio-tracking studies dating back as far as the early 1980s have shown early season muskies suspended over open water. In lakes with populations of cool-water forage like ciscoes, late spring and early summer, before lakes stratify and thermoclines develop, can be one of the best open-water bites of the year. With cool water temperatures, ciscoes remain high in the water column, and muskies take advantage of their availability. Even lakes without lots of ciscoes can sometimes produce good open-water bites. During late springs, when weed growth is underdeveloped, schools of other types of baitfish such as small sunfish or crappies may suspend out in open water, often just below the surface. Muskies need baitfish

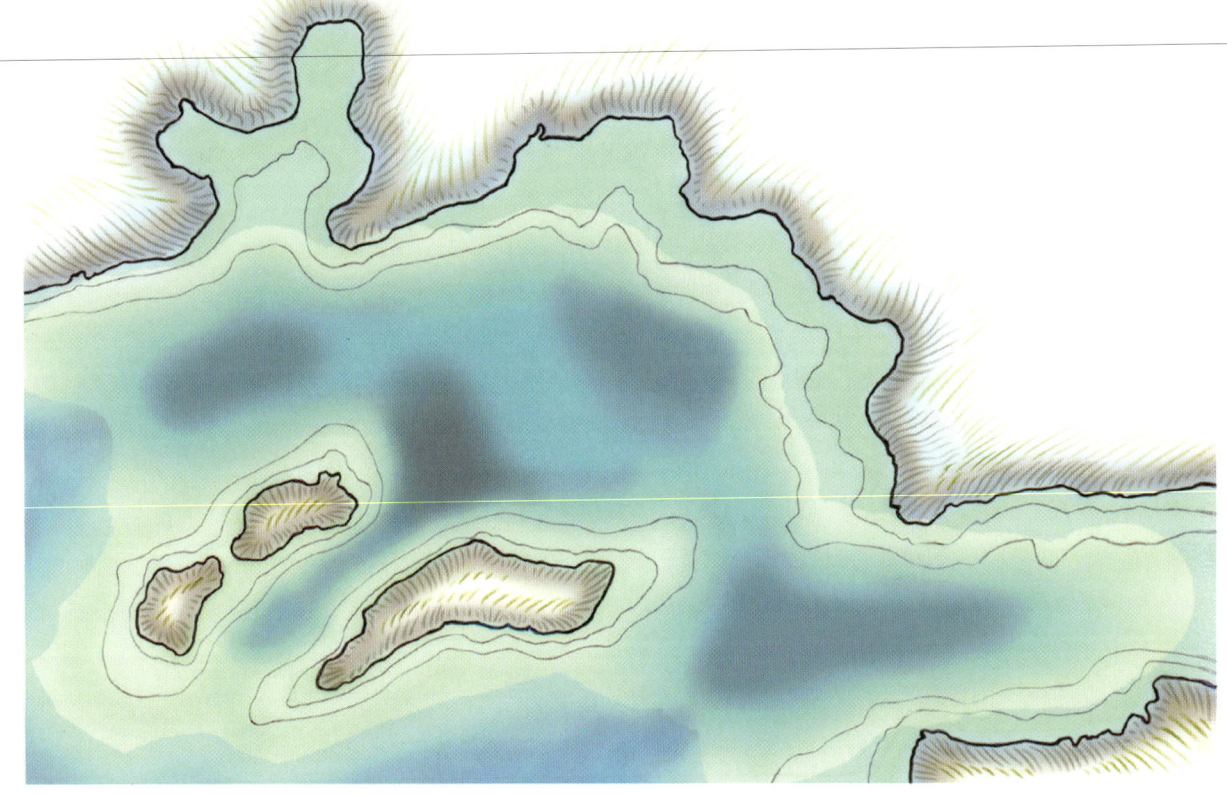

more than they need structure. Given the choice—baitfish or structure—muskies choose baitfish every time.

Especially in spring, look for areas of confined open water rather than vast main lake basins. Confined open water can be deeper holes within large bays, the first deep water off the break in front of spawning flats or bays, off the tips of points, around the edges of nearby reefs, or deep flats between large points. Muskies aren't holding *on* structure but still seem to relate to it somewhat, often staying within a few hundred yards.

Finding open-water muskies at this time of year can be a challenge. Good electronics are essential, but often muskies and baitfish high in the water column will spook off to the side as your boat passes over them, so you won't mark them on a graph. Loons or seagulls feeding over open water can clue you in to the presence of baitfish, but often you just need to go try it.

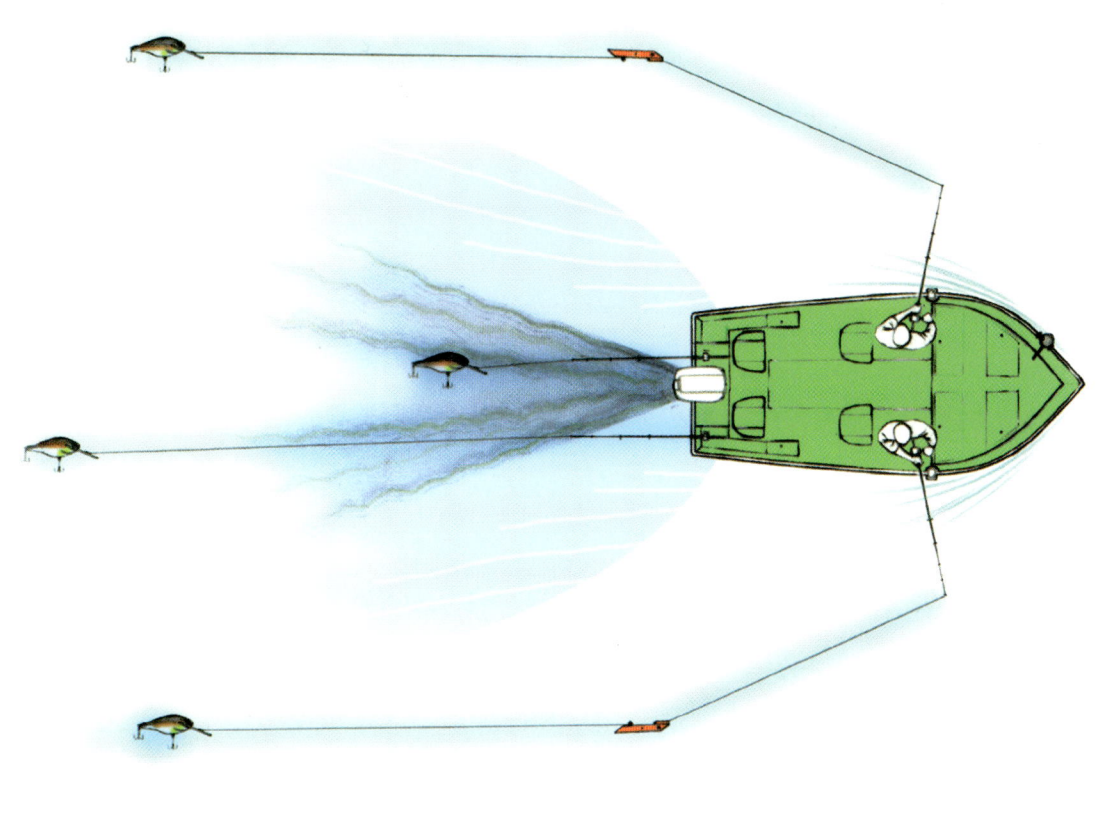

If a certain type of weed edge or structure produces a muskie just outside spawning bay #1, then be sure to look for the same combination of factors outside spawning bay #2. That is not to say that you should *only* fish structures that mimic the hot ones. Not by a long shot. Fish every viable spot thoroughly—shallow, deep, inside, outside. But structural elements that look like the one that produced your last muskie give you a starting point in each new area and can help you narrow down the search. Common sense.

Searching Efficiently—Presentation

The best way to check out all these different types of spots—and eventually narrow down your search—is to cover water quickly. There are several search bait options, including in-line bucktails, spinnerbaits, and topwater lures. For searching purposes, the lures should be easy to quickly retrieve. In-line bucktails with French-style blades like a Blue Fox Muskie Buck or Shumway Funky Chicken; compact, light, high-riding baits like a Musky Mania Lilly Tail; or heavy-bladed, high-flash baits like the Windels Muskie Harasser are classic search baits if the weeds are down. Spinnerbaits like Rad Dogs and Grinders, in a compact 1- to 1½-ounce size are nearly perfect search baits. Change their blades from standard #8 Colorado or fluted Indiana blades to smaller #6 or #7 Colorados. They'll be easier to fish quickly, and won't pull nearly as hard (a definite plus early in the season when casting muscles aren't quite in shape yet.) Spinnerbaits are virtually weedless and can be fluttered/dropped into weed pockets or fished deep along edges like a jig-spin (which is what they are).

Topwaters make excellent search baits when the water is warm and the muskies are aggressive. Straight-retrieve topwaters, such as tail or head spinners like the Rumbler or the Musky Buster Top Walker, or smaller, more subtle propbaits like a Mouldy's Topper Stopper can be worked faster than walk-the-dog topwaters, so you can cover more water.

After a few hours—or a day—of fishing a lot of spots, and sampling different types of spots, you will start to get a handle on which stage of the transition the muskies are in, and have some ideas about where to focus your attention. If you have been lucky enough to see some big muskies (follows, near misses, maybe even a caught fish or two), then you're ready. It's time to get serious.

Now, instead of trying to cover a lot of water, you can fish known big fish spots more thoroughly. Spend enough time on a spot to fish it at all depths, poke and probe every edge and inside turn, present lures fast and slow. You can go back to a big muskie spot at sunset, as a front approaches, at the crack of dawn, at night. And you can fish the "pattern." If points outside bays #1, #2, and #3 produce nice muskies. Then why not check out the points outside bays #4, #5, #6, etc.? Why resist the urge?

The point is that the first 10 to 20 percent of your early-season muskie outing should be aimed at determining which stage of the transition the muskies are in. The remaining time can be spent using that knowledge to catch the fish you're really after.

Other Presentation Options

Ideally, all you'll need to catch early season muskies is a few bucktails, a spinnerbait or two, and maybe a few topwaters, just for fun. Often enough though, weather and water conditions can require a change in tactics if you're going to catch fish. Sometimes that's bad news. Other times, it's great news.

Cold, late springs, clear water, and turned-off fish can mean needing to slow down and downsize your lures. If fish spawned fairly recently, smaller males are often most active and catchable in spring, and larger females may simply be unwilling to chase larger lures at all. In clear, cold water, the most catchable fish are often extremely shallow, and very spooky. Using a 5-ounce lure in those conditions is sort of like throwing a cinderblock into a swimming pool. Every fish within 50 feet will scatter. Small, light, bass-size tackle lets you present your lures softly and naturally. Even big muskies sometimes make mistakes if you sneak up on them.

Small, ⅜- to ¾-ounce spinnerbaits like Northland Reed Runners, matched with a flipping stick and 20- to 25-pound-test monofilament, allow you to make long casts to quickly search shallow sand or mudflats and shallow weeds. Minnow baits like Bomber Long-As, 6-inch Jakes, or Rapala Husky Jerks worked with subtle twitches or pulls and long pauses can also trigger reluctant fish—or at least get them to follow and reveal their location so that you can try them again later when conditions improve.

Finally, jigs with plastics like a Bait Rigs Esox Cobra Jig tipped with

Early-season fishing may require adjusting lure size to match conditions. Upsize baits (left column, top to bottom): 10-inch Believer, 10-inch Suick, Magnum Windels Harasser. Downsize baits (right column, top to bottom): Northland Magnum Reed Runner, Musky Mania 6-inch Squirrely Jake, American Hardwoods Lac Seul Mini, Bait Rigs Esox Cobra Jig. DAVE OLSON

Reaper tail or Berkley Power Lizard have caught a lot of 50-inch muskies early in the season. On clear, calm days, you may even be able to sight fish. Slowly and quietly cruise shallow sand flats, mud-bottomed bays, or sheltered shorelines near spawning areas, and look for muskies sunning themselves on the bottom. Good polarized sunglasses are essential. When you spot a fish, cast well beyond it, carefully scoot the jig along the bottom until it's in front of the fish, then simply let it sit, subtly shaking it once in a while. At least sometimes, they'll swim over, roll on their side, and simply pick the jig off the bottom. It's a method that takes a lot of patience, but it's exciting when it works. For covering larger areas, a ½-ounce Esox Cobra Jig with a silicone skirt and a large twin-tail grub can be fished extremely slowly by swimming it steadily, with occasional pauses to let the jig flutter briefly. It's a subtle, nonthreatening presentation that's very effective during tough conditions. In one early-season Wisconsin tournament, all thirty-nine muskies caught were caught on jigs. That is why a lot of pros go small in the spring.

On the other end of the spectrum, if the water is warmer and weeds are up, conventional muskie gear and tactics are obviously an option. Warmer water and perhaps a longer period of recovery from the spawn due to an early spring can mean muskies with a metabolism that's fairly cranked up. With thicker weeds for cover, and slightly lower visibility even on generally clear lakes as plankton and algae develop in the warmer water, muskies are less spooky. The splash of a larger lure will be just as likely to attract an aggressive muskie as repel it. Combine all that with a lack of fishing pressure, and the combination of factors can make conditions like these a great opportunity for a big fish.

Throughout the day with conditions like this, it's hard to beat simply snapping on a bucktail and firing away. Flashy, fast-moving baits with large willow blades like Windels Harassers or Northland Bionic Bucktails hook well, trigger aggressive fish, and nothing's more efficient for covering water. Bucktails also figure-eight exceptionally well; and unpressured, aggressive fish are often very vulnerable to a well-executed figure eight this time of year. It's probably your best shot of the season at catching a big fish at boatside.

Bucktails are good tools for not only catching fish but also locating larger fish you can return to later, at prime times like dusk or dawn. Large, big-fish lures are a logical choice when you are returning to a big fish that followed your fast-moving bucktail earlier in the day. When you go back to that 4-footer at dusk, slow-moving, tantalizing targets can trigger an explosive strike.

Good choices include jerkbaits like a 9-inch Suick or 8-inch Reef Hawg or shallow-running crankbaits like an 8-inch Believer. Larger, big-bladed bucktails like an Eagle Tail, double-bladed bulger bucktails like a Shumway Flasher, and tandem spinnerbaits like the M&G and the tandem Rad Dog fool a lot of big muskies, too. When fishing shallow spring spots, these large muskie lures are especially effective on mesotrophic Canadian Shield lakes, like Lac Seul and Lake of the Woods.

When muskies are over open water early in the season, the strategies for finding them and catching them are still the same—cover water efficiently—but the technique is often quite different. Where it's legal, trolling is often the best approach.

Early-season open-water muskies are often found fairly high in the water column. Sometimes they're almost on the surface. These fish often spook out to the sides as a boat passes overhead, so getting lures out away from the boat with in-line planer boards (or a mast and ski system, if you're set up for it) is definitely a plus.

Troll through potential areas at speeds ranging from 2 to 4 miles per hour. Vary your speed, and make frequent S-turns as you troll. Turns, together with any wave action, cause your lures to change speed and direction, an important trigger when trolling.

Many lures work well for open-water trolling: crankbaits, some jerkbaits, even topwaters at times. Behind boards, crankbaits like 6- and 8-inch Jakes (sometimes 10-inchers in warmer water), Drifter Super Stalkers, 8-inch Believers running on the shallow setting or set close behind boards, Musky Mania Ernies and Little Ernies, Esox Research Company's Triple-D and Double-D crankbaits, and Bomber Long-A's can all be productive. Vary the amount of line behind the board to experiment with running depth. Focus most of your effort in the top 10 to 12 feet of the water column, however, unless you're marking baitfish or muskies deeper on your electronics.

If you have a third person in the boat, or multiple lines are legal where you're fishing, the same lures described above, run on a flat line 70 to 120 feet behind the boat, can work. Finally, especially on overcast or windy days, an erratic jerkbait like a weighted Sledge run just off the transom in the prop wash—between 10 and 30 feet behind the boat—can be amazingly effective at times. It works, and hooking a big muskie at 3 miles per hour with 15 feet of line out is definitely exciting.

Early-season postspawn fishing occurs in a period of rapid transition. For that reason, much of this chapter has focused on timing and searching. Our challenge is understanding the timing of ice-out, spring weather patterns, the muskies' spawning and recovery, and their transition into more stable summer locations

Opposite: Early-season lures for Lake of the Woods and other Canadian Shield waters, top to bottom: Ruff Tackle Rad Dog, Blue Fox Musky Buck, 9-inch Suick, Drifter Tackle 10-inch Believer. DAVE OLSON

Early-season open-water trolling baits, top to bottom: Sledgehammer Lures Sledge, Bomber Long-A, Drifter Super Stalker, Musky Mania 8-inch Jake. DAVE OLSON

and habits. Searching and learning is how we connect with those fish in transition.

In the next seasonal phase, there is less guesswork. But there are plenty of challenges—and some fantastic muskie fishing.

On to summer…

CHAPTER SEVEN

Summer Peak
(July in the northern tier)

The theme of the summer peak is peak feeding, peak weed growth, and rising water temperatures. It is also a time of peak fishing pressure and peak boat traffic.

Some of these factors come together to produce one of the best bites of the year, for both numbers and for big fish. Other factors influence our tactics and techniques.

We are now well past the time it takes big muskies to recover from spawning. And the warming water temperatures are kicking the muskie's metabolism into high gear. Feeding is just about all they have in mind.

If the muskies in your waters rely on weeds for cover and ambush, the healthy weedbeds of July give them everything they need. And these crisp green weeds are also fairly easy to fish through. So far, it's all good. But our tactical decisions must also take into consideration the presence of other anglers—often, a lot of other anglers.

Tactical Factors

When a top predator like a muskie encounters heavy fishing pressure, it quickly learns that there is a bigger, badder predator on the water. In order to survive and thrive, even just to live and eat in peace without getting into brawls with folks in boats, muskies adapt. If their natural prime feeding areas are getting pounded by boat after boat of muskie anglers, many muskies will make adjustments in their location and in their feeding times. The adjustments may be fairly small, like dropping down a little deeper into the sanctuary of thicker weeds. Or they may be fairly large, like moving from a heavily fished weedbed to a small grassy patch on the top of a deep hump in the middle of the lake. We're not saying that muskies make "logical" or "thoughtful" adjustments, but more of a natural reaction to harassment that evolution has bred into the current race of survivors.

In another example, muskies that have "learned" to respond to heavy fishing pressure or even high levels of peak summer boat traffic by feeding at night are likely to be an underfished and unscarred portion of that lake's muskie population. As the muskies adapt, so must you.

Tactics and Techniques

The best way to handle a lot of fishing pressure is to avoid it. If everyone is doing one thing, then do something else. If everyone is fishing one area, then fish somewhere else. There are many ways to go against the grain, and most of them lead to catching more and bigger muskies.

If everyone else is fishing obvious classic weedbeds or classic reefs (primary spots), then maybe the muskies have moved off to secondary, less classic, spots—spots that are less obvious or less easy to fish.

If you can find spots that are not heavily fished, yet have good healthy weedbeds or a combination of weeds and rocks, then you can really have some fun.

Presentations for Fishing Shallow Summer Muskies

During summer peak, water temperatures are rising, and the muskies' metabolisms are in full gear. They're feeding regularly, so there's no need to pick-pick away at spots with slow-moving baits. When you're dealing with minimal fishing pressure, there's no reason not to just get after them with something fast moving, cover spots quickly, and move on. Will slower presentations catch fish? Definitely. But during summer peak, slow presentations that excel at triggering reluctant muskies just don't cover enough water. Get your lure in front of as many muskies as possible, and find the active ones.

Fast-moving, horizontal presentations like topwaters and bucktails are ideal for this style of fishing. Bucktails like the Musky Mania Lilly Tail, the Northland Bionic Bucktail, or the Windels Harasser cast easily, hook fish exceptionally well, and can be fished fast over the tops of shallow weeds and rocks.

Fast-moving topwaters are also exceptional search lures during summer peak. Topwaters can call fish in from a considerable distance, and it's hard to imagine something more fun. Tail-spinning topwaters like the Rumbler or Lac Seul Turr-bo from American Hardwoods Lures can be fished quickly to cover a lot of water and are noisy enough to draw fish even in wind and waves. Buzzbaits like the Ruff Tackle Buzz Dog or CJ's Buzzer are also good options.

In between traditional bucktails and topwaters are the bulgers—hybrid baits that do a little of the best of both lure styles. Bulgers like the Professional Edge Krook and Bruce Shumway's Flasher ride high in the water column, waking or bulging the surface like a topwater, but still have the flash, vibration and—most important—excellent hooking ability of a traditional bucktail. Especially at dawn and dusk, bulgers are excellent search lures and exceptional as "throwback" lures to fish that have followed other lures.

In-line bucktails excel for efficiently covering water and finding aggressive fish during summer peak. Top to bottom: Blue Fox Musky Buck, Professional Edge Krook, Windels Harasser, Shumway Flasher. DAVE OLSON

Fishing fast with high-speed search lures is fine when fishing pressure is low—or when searching acres of secondary water.

But when your lake consists of nothing but high-pressure "community" spots, you will need to fish the spots differently. There is a strong temptation to fish quickly, to rush around and beat the other guy to a spot. Not so fast. Fishing quickly with topwaters and in-line bucktails gives you shallow, two-dimensional coverage of each spot. Aggressive muskies will rise up to the surface to attack shallow-running lures. But pressured muskies may be hunkered down deeper in the weeds or in the nooks and crannies of a large weed/rock complex. To reach these fish, you need to go down to them. Instead of trying to cover a lot of water, fish those well known big-fish spots more thoroughly. Spend enough time on a spot to fish it at all depths, to poke and probe every edge and inside turn, to present lures fast and slow.

One of the best lures for this is the spinnerbait. A single-bladed spinnerbait can be retrieved quickly to cover shallow water, but it can

Short-arm, single-spin spinnerbaits are the best option for fishing deep in heavy weeds. Top to bottom: Ruff Tackle Rad Dog, Esox Research Company Grinder. DAVE OLSON

also be fluttered down into pockets in the weeds and into gaps between boulders. A spinnerbait can be "slow-rolled" deep over midlake humps and along walls and edges. Using a spinnerbait as a deeper running lure—as a tool that can cover all depths and slide over most obstacles—will put you in contact with muskies that most other people on the water never see.

The only downside to spinnerbaits is that you have to keep them moving. You can let them drop a bit, because the blade keeps working on the fall. But generally you must keep them moving at least fast enough to keep the blade thumping. There is no suspending or hovering in place with a spinnerbait. Motionless pauses are not an option. But sometimes a suspended motionless pause is exactly what you want.

Surprisingly, 10-inch Believers, Suicks, and Bobbie Baits can be very effectively fished in the weeds. It helps if the weeds are green and crisp. That's why the summer peak is a perfect time to use them.

A 10-inch Believer is a somewhat bulky, wide-wobbling, banana-style crankbait. Originally intended for trolling, the Believer has two connection eyelets—one for deep trolling and one for shallow. On the shallow connection, the Believer is also an effective bait for fishing healthy green weedbeds. It is very buoyant, so it can be retrieved slowly, breaking the water's surface like a topwater. As the lure passes over pockets in the weeds, you can drive it down with a quick turn of the reel handle or a downward twitch of the rod. The key is to cast to a gap in the surface weeds and then slowly steer the lure with your rod and nurse it back to the boat with pauses, wobbles, and changes of direction. Strikes are ferocious.

Suicks and Bobbie Baits are two jerkbaits that can also be finessed and steered through weeds. There is no built-in wobble, like the Believer has, so retrieves are a series of rod jerks and turns of the reel handle. But instead of long, hard pulls to drive the lure deep, the finessing consists of light taps and brief turns of the reel. When you see the lure enter a pocket or a lane in the weeds, drive the lure down with a longer, harder pull.

Using treble-hooked lures in weeds sounds like a bad idea, but these select baits fish exceptionally well in and over weeds. Top to bottom: Schutt's Sledge, 10-inch Suick, Bobbie Bait, Drifter Tackle 10-inch Believer. DAVE OLSON

But then stop for a moment and let the lure rise slowly. Suicks and Bobbies actually seem to back up out of a weed clump if you give them a chance. It's on that slow rise or dead pause that many strikes occur. Be ready.

When fishing jerkbaits this way, a waterlogged or slightly weighted lure that rises very slowly will produce more strikes.

Fishing the Slop

One of the classic hard-to-fish types of spots is dense weeds, commonly referred to as "slop." Unlike open clean weeds with a lot of nice pretty pockets and lanes to cast into, slop is a virtually impenetrable mat of weeds. It is just flat out hard to fish. So most people fish around the edge of the slop and then move on to the next spot. That's good for us, because they are reinforcing some muskies' impression that thick weeds are a sanctuary. If we are willing to get in there and pay the price, we will often find some fairly naïve and aggressive fish. Being willing is one thing. Doing is another. There are some tricks to it. Start with the lures.

A spinnerbait is the basic tool for fishing slop. Well-built spinnerbaits with short heavy-wire arms (such as Rad Dogs and Grinders) will handle most weedy situations. A 1-ounce spinnerbait with a large Colorado blade can be crawled through and over some fairly dense weeds. And a 2- or 3-ounce Grinder with a willowleaf blade can be fished down into and under the weeds, with the right technique (see "Grinding" in chapter 3).

But sometimes the slop is just too nasty for a spinnerbait. In these situations, a determined angler will switch to less-traditional baits. Weedless spoons are universally associated with fishing for pike in weeds. Spoons are also one of the most overlooked/ignored lures in muskie fishing. This is just plain silly. In some areas of the muskie world, spoons routinely catch muskies. They have for generations. Muskies are muskies. If Pennsylvania muskies can be routinely caught on spoons, then why not Wisconsin muskies? A muskie-size Johnson Silver Minnow with a pork rind or plastic trailer is probably the best tool for fishing slop ever made. For slower presentations, large weightless soft plastics like a Texas-rigged 9-inch Lunker City Slugg-o or Yum Dinger can be pitched into small pockets, then skittered over solid mats of weeds.

But it takes more than just the right lures to effectively fish slop. Rods should be long and heavy power. Long rods (8 feet or more) make it easier to control the path of your lure. If you need to make your lure come over an obstacle, or if you want to steer it around a clump of moss, a long rod helps. Hooking and playing a 4-foot muskie in heavy weeds requires heavy power just to have a chance. It also requires at least 80-pound no-stretch line and a winch of a reel, like the Ambassadeur 7000.

Another thing that discourages most people from getting into a large tangled weedbed is boat control. The outboard should be tilted up so you don't drag half the weedbed on your prop. And the electric trolling motor is often rendered useless by thick slop. This is one of those times when a fairly stiff wind can be your friend. Tilt your outboard up and take a drift through the weedbed. If it's calm, it's time to dig out those paddles that you thought were only for emergencies. Better yet, carry a push-pole. Yes it's hard fishing. That's why few people do it well. And that's why slop is a sanctuary for big muskies.

Lures, rods, reels, line, navigation in the slop, and a determination to fish where others fear to tread … that's a start. But there is a trick to it, too. Start with short 20-foot casts. Short, precise casts do a number of things for you. They let you hit a specific target and, more importantly, miss a hazard, such as a clump of moss that would kill the cast. Short casts and short retrieves give you a better chance to land a big muskie. It's tough enough fishing without having to reel 80 pounds of weeds as your muskie swims and jumps 100 feet out on the end of a long cast. And this last reason is critical. To fish in true slop means routinely picking weeds off your bait. If you cast 100 feet and pick up weeds after 10 feet of retrieve, then a 100-foot retrieve is almost completely wasted. But a 20-foot cast with 10 feet of clean retrieve, and then another and another … Make four or five 20-foot casts in the time it takes for one 100-foot cast. Even if the weeds are bad, 50 percent of your total retrieve distance is clean. With the

FISH HEAVY SLOP DURING COLD FRONTS

Many large muskies have been caught in the slop under bright, windy cold-front conditions. If you find a big thick (slop) weedbed under windy cold-front conditions, you have probably found a muskie sanctuary.

Let the wind do the work. Position your boat outside the weedbed to set up a drift through the middle of the bed. Tilt the outboard up and leave your trolling motor out of the water. Then just take the drift. If necessary, tweak the direction of the drift with a boat paddle. Cast away. As usual in the slop, keep your casts very short and precise.

The muskies, safe and secure in their sanctuary, could be the most catchable fish in the lake.

100-foot cast, only 10 percent of your total retrieve distance is clean. The people who understand this trick catch most of the fish. The people who don't, usually give up—because it isn't easy.

Summer Fishing on Oligotrophic Lakes

On mesotrophic (moderately fertile) lakes, weeds and even slop are muskie magnets in this summer peak period. But what about the colder, more-sterile oligotrophic lakes?

Note: Oligotrophic lakes often harbor a lake trout population, but not always. So oligotrophic lakes are frequently referred to by the more easily pronounceable name "lake trout lakes," even though it's a misnomer in many instances.

Because lake trout (type) lakes are deeper and colder and have few weeds even at their peak, timing and location are much different from mesotrophic lakes. On many of the larger, deeper lakes in northwest Ontario, postspawn muskies disperse out to deep basins, where they feed on open-water baitfish. These relatively sterile lakes have a very low muskie population to begin with. Dispersal can turn them into a needle-in-a-haystack affair. In short, the early summer peak may not be a muskie-fishing peak on the larger trout waters. The best time to fish these lakes is often later in summer—and again in the very late fall, when these muskies tend to bunch up.

The best trout lakes to fish in July are the ones that are smaller and more manageable, preferably single-basin lakes.

One of the best reasons to fish trout water at this time (or any other) is the size of the muskies. Another thing to keep in mind is a relative lack of fishing pressure. Most anglers are looking for action. Few have the patience to trade a lot of muskie action for one monster fish. What low fishing pressure means for us is that we can fish the classic, obvious muskie spots. If a spot on a trout lake is big and complex and has everything you are looking for (we call it a "designer spot"), then fish it.

On the smaller lakes you can fairly easily fish most of the contact points that rise out of the basin. You can fish the largest, most complex reefs, points, island saddles—any transition from the main lake basin to shallow water.

Clear, sterile water calls for several adjustments in tactics and technique. In clear water, light penetrates a lot deeper, and the fish are more aware of your presence. You should fish deeper—at least to the lake's Secchi disk depth. In clear water muskies can easily see your lures. They can see when a lure looks phony or boring, so they are harder to startle into a reaction strike. Try slightly smaller versions of your favorite lures. Use natural colors (cisco, perch, sucker patterns, or all black). That said, sometimes chartreuse or hot-red blades on black spinnerbaits and bucktails are very effective. Work your lures faster than you would on darker waters. They can see it coming a long way off. Don't give them time to "decide." Try to make them react.

Because weeds are rare, fish any deep weeds you find. Find a point, a boulder reef, or a deep saddle with a small clump of weeds. Run a spinnerbait through them. Let it flutter down into the base of the weeds. Then point your rod at the lure and reel quickly. Run a deep-diving crankbait along the edges of the boulders. Under ideal conditions (a bit of wind, heavy overcast, sunset), come back and work a jerkbait over the structure. Or a topwater. For some reason, walk-the-dog topwaters and jerkbaits, like the Doc and Reef Hawg, respectively, are very effective at drawing muskies up from the depths. This presentation must look like an easy, vulnerable meal from down below. Or maybe it's just an irritation and makes a muskie want to crush it.

Many of the tactics and techniques that work on the more common mesotrophic waters work equally well—with minor adjustments—on trout lakes. Muskies are muskies. But due to factors like forage base, weed growth, light penetration, and water temperature, the timing of their transitions and their relative location will differ. The only way to narrow it down from there is on the water.

CHAPTER EIGHT

Mid- to Late Summer
(August in the northern tier)

The mid- to late-summer period is a time of stability. Water temperatures plateau, usually in the low- to mid-70-degree range in northern latitudes, weed growth is fully developed, and a broad range of forage species are well into their summer routines.

For muskies, the mid- to late summer period is a continuation of the patterns established during summer peak, although at a steadier pace. Research has shown that on many waters, muskies establish definite home ranges and simply never leave them throughout this entire period. One biologist has said that home range boundaries were so pronounced they were "like the fences around a farmer's field." Fish just don't cross them. Within those ranges, muskies are feeding steadily as warm water temperatures bring their metabolic rates to seasonal peaks.

For muskie anglers, this time of stability is both good news and bad news. Muskies are in fairly predictable locations, so finding them often isn't the challenge on most waters. But summer also brings environmental and social factors that can make mid- to late summer a challenge—the classic Dog Days.

One factor is fishing pressure. Mid- to late summer is peak vacation time, and classic, obvious spots get pounded incessantly. Muskies are the apex predator in their environment and will, given the choice, set up on the "best" locations in a body of water. But fishing pressure can change that. There's little doubt—based not only on practical experience but also significant fisheries research—that fish respond negatively to fishing pressure. They just don't like being fished for. They may respond to that pressure in a variety of ways. They may remain in the same location but become unresponsive to commonly used presentation techniques and popular lures unless conditions are absolutely perfect and fish are extremely active. They may change their daily routines to avoid periods of high pressure by feeding early in the morning, or at night. They may relocate altogether, moving away from obvious and thus highly pressured spots to less-obvious secondary structure that, while not ideal in other respects, offers the security of less fishing pressure.

As summer progresses, environmental factors like algae blooms, changes in weed growth, and high water temperatures can also complicate the picture on some bodies of water.

Algae blooms can turn some lakes into pea-green swamps during mid- to late summer, drastically cutting visibility in the upper water column. How much a bloom actually affects the fish is highly debatable, but it can definitely affect an angler's efficiency and confidence when a fluorescent-orange lure disappears into the green 4 inches down. As summer progresses, weedbeds can become overgrown and filled with stringy "junk weeds" or, on highly fertile bodies of water like the mesotrophic portion of Lake of the Woods, become matted with filamentous algae. In either case, weedbeds can become difficult if not impossible to fish through. In the southern portion of the muskies' range, or during extreme heat spells in the North, high water temperatures can shut fish down—even make fishing for muskies at all ethically questionable due to the risk of delayed mortality when releasing fish in very hot water.

Generally, though, if you are able to adapt to conditions, whether social influences like fishing pressure or environmental factors like algae blooms, mid- to late summer can be a period of steady, if not spectacular, fishing success.

Tactics and Techniques

Under ideal conditions and absent any of the challenging factors described above, mid- to late-summer muskies aren't complicated. Overall, fish are feeding fairly steadily, and day-to-day fish mood is largely determined by local weather conditions. A cold front can put them off for a few days, while an oncoming storm can crank up the activity. A straightforward approach of classic techniques—high-efficiency, good-hooking lures like bucktails and fast-moving topwaters under good weather conditions and more-deliberate presentations like jerkbaits, jigs, twitched crankbaits, or slow-rolled spinnerbaits after a front—is a good basis to start from. Adjust lure selection based on cover conditions, depth, or water clarity.

Spinnerbait Trolling

On many bodies of water, much of the activity during the summer period may be centered on large weed flats. Large weed flats provide cover and forage—and hold lots of muskies. On bigger bodies of water, major weedbeds can be huge. Even on smaller lakes, major flats can range from 4 feet on the inside edge to 12 to 17 feet on the outside edge, depending on water clarity. Each edge has points and fingers, small inside turns and patches of thicker or thinner weed growth. On the flat itself are thicker clumps of weeds, open pockets, transitions between weed types, and other features like isolated rock piles or changes in bottom content. On a map, a weed flat can appear as a uniform piece of structure. Consider weed flats in terms of where fish may be holding, however, and they become a complex jumble of mini-spots. Any of these elements—inside and outside edges, or on the flat itself—can hold mid- to late-summer muskies. On a given day, fish may be concentrated on one area of the flat, like the outside edge, or scattered across the entire flat.

Fishing a large flat, even with fast-moving baits like bucktails, can be very time-consuming. Where trolling is allowed, spinnerbait trolling can be the most efficient means of thoroughly covering massive flats. Tandem spinnerbaits such as the Ruff Tackle Heavy Tandem Rad Dog, the Lindy M&G Tandem, or, for deeper edges, the 5-ounce ERC Grinder can be trolled over weed flats at speeds that range from 3 to 5 miles per hour.

Spinnerbait trolling isn't complex. There are, though, a few technical details that make it different from most other muskie-trolling techniques.

Trolling spinnerbaits, clockwise from top right: Ruff Tackle Rad Dog, Esox Research Company Grinder, Shumway Funky Chicken, Northland Bionic Bucktail. DAVE OLSON

Most significant is rod choice. For most trolling applications, soft rods that absorb the shock of a muskie strike are the norm. For spinnerbaits, though, a stiffer rod, more along the lines of a typical bucktail rod in power and action, is required. Contacting cover and ripping the tops of weeds is an important part of spinnerbait trolling, and soft rods that load slowly will pull weeds loose rather than snapping through them, leading to constantly fouled lures. Though it's not a necessity, a line-counter reel like a Shimano Tekota 600LC makes adjusting line lengths more accurate. Whatever reel you choose, a smooth drag is an absolute must.

A key to trolling spinnerbaits successfully is maintaining running depth of the spinnerbait so that it occasionally ticks the tops of the weeds. Crankbait running depth is determined for the most part by lure design and distance behind the boat. With spinnerbaits, speed controls depth. Higher speed increases lift from the blades, bringing the bait higher in the water. Slow down, and the lure runs deeper. It's a simple concept, but learning to control running depth with the throttle can take some practice. Although short line trolling spinnerbaits can be effective at times, running baits 80 to 100 feet back is more versatile in terms of controlling running depth. Watch your electronics, and adjust your speed to drop the spinnerbait deeper over lower growing weeds, or accelerate to hop it over taller clumps. Contacting cover is an important triggering tool for trolled spinnerbaits. Watch your rod tip, and accelerate just as you make contact with the weed tops at the tips of points or around thicker clumps of weeds. The bait rises as you accelerate, and rips through the weed tops. Most hits happen just as the bait clears the weeds.

Night Fishing

Mid- to late summer can be one of the best times of the season for night fishing. Fish may shift to after-dark activity patterns for a variety of reasons.

Fishing pressure and general boating traffic are two possible causes. Forage activity patterns may also play a role in shifting things to a night bite. Twilight vertical movement of pelagic species like ciscoes can trigger periods of activity at and just after dark (or just before dawn) that can carry over into the first few hours of full dark. Other forage species like bullheads or suckers may increase their activity after dark, while perch and panfish reduce theirs, but become more vulnerable due to their inability to see well after dark. Whatever the case, on some bodies of water the night bite can be the best thing going during the summer months.

In the past, the rule of thumb for selecting night lakes was to look for clear bodies of water with a lot of fishing pressure or boat traffic. Today we know that muskies can be active at night on a variety of different kinds of systems, even fairly dark-water lakes with lower fishing pressure. Only some experimenting will tell you if there's an opportunity for muskies after dark on your favorite lake.

MUSKIES UNDER THE MOON—OR NOT

Which moon phases are best for night muskies, and whether moonlight helps or hurts night fishing is a subject of some debate among muskie anglers. There's no clear consensus, but some interesting anecdotal evidence suggests there's a difference between Leech Lake–strain muskies and Wisconsin-strain muskies when it comes to the moon/no moon question. Rob's experience on Minnesota lakes with Leech Lake–strain muskies has been that no-moon or dark-of-the-moon periods are far superior to full moonlight for muskies after dark. Leech Lake area guide and *The Next Bite—Esox Angler* writer Dan Craven has made similar observations based on experiences on several Minnesota muskie lakes. Several Wisconsin anglers, however, have described the opposite experience—or at least no preference for dark-of-the-moon or moonless nights.

By necessity, night fishing requires a simplified approach. Everything, from navigation to presentation to boat control, gets more difficult after dark. Clean your boat. Put away anything you aren't going to need, like extra rods or lures, and make sure release tools are someplace where you can easily find them.

Headlamps are obviously a must. A few years ago, headlamps were bulky, heavy, and unpleasant to wear. LED bulbs have changed that. Lamps now are bright and weigh next to nothing, and wearing them can be as simple as clipping them to the bill of a cap. Besides headlamps, a spotlight can be handy for navigating or landing and unhooking fish. Night is also definitely a time to consider pinching the barbs down on all your hooks. It makes releasing fish much easier, and it's a lot safer if you happen to get hooked while releasing them.

Lure selection for night fishing is simplified, too. Slow-moving topwaters are the classic night presentation, and large topwaters like the Ti-Foon or Giant Klunker from American Hardwood Lures or giant creepers like the Wave Walker from Musky Buster retrieved at a slow, steady pace can certainly work. But hooking percentages for topwaters are fairly low even during daylight, and things don't improve much after dark. There are definitely more options besides topwaters for night muskies. In fact, the full range of muskie lures—even soft plastics—will catch muskies after dark. However, a few lure types do stand out as night baits.

Big bucktails, especially large double-bladed models like the Cowgirl from Musky Mayhem, the Musky Mojo Triple-X, or Bruce Shumway's Magnum Flasher are perhaps the most efficient after-dark bait, and are definitely better hooking baits than topwaters. Tandem spinnerbaits like CJ's or Tandem Rad Dog also excel at night.

Large-profile crankbaits like 10-inch Jakes and Believers work, too. Believers are most often retrieved at a steady pace, but Jakes can be worked with a stop-and-go or twitch-and-pause retrieve as well. The old rule of thumb that slow and steady was the only retrieve for after dark just isn't true. Muskies have no trouble catching twitched crankbaits. Or jerkbaits. Using jerkbaits after dark flies in the face of tradition. But there are times—especially under the same conditions where you'd use jerkbaits during the day, like tough conditions or after cold fronts—when jerkbaits will out produce any other bait after dark. Jerkbaits with rattles, like Musky Mania Burts, are good, but large-profile gliders like Reef Hawgs or 10-inch Suicks work, too.

Lures for the night shift, clockwise from top right: Musky Mania Burt, Drifter Tackle 10-inch Believer, American Hardwoods Lac Seul Giant, American Hardwoods Giant Klunker, Lindy M/G, Shumway Flasher, Musky Mayhem Cowgirl.
DAVE OLSON

Night fishing is one exception to our general rule on not doing a figure eight after each cast. At a minimum, you should do at least one full figure eight or oval at the end of each retrieve. Adding small strips of glow tape to lures you plan to use after dark to help you spot them as they near the boat so you know when to begin an "8" is a must. Just a small strip down the back of crankbaits or jerkbaits is all that's needed. Another option, and one we actually prefer, is adding a glow bead to the line just above the leader. Not only does it help you spot the leader coming in, but it also helps keep you from smashing the swivel into your rod tip, which gets tough on the top guide.

Adding lots of glow to lures with glow tape or paint, or putting glow blades on bucktails or spinnerbaits, seems like a logical idea. In reality, it doesn't help much. In fact, too much glow seems to do more harm than good. (Although glow blades on spinnerbaits will definitely catch bass at night. Lots of bass.) Muskies just don't seem to like too much glow. If your instincts tell you glow is necessary to help fish find your lure after dark, consider how many glow-in-the-dark perch or ciscoes are paddling around. Muskies can find lures just fine, glow or not.

Locations for night muskies are similar to those during the day, at least generally speaking. A frequent misconception about night muskies is that it's primarily a shallow water pattern. Certainly on some lakes it is. But that's most often true where muskies are shallow during the day as well, whether that's on shallow reefs, sand flats, or shallow weedbeds. If deeper spots like deep reefs or humps or deep weedlines are the main pattern during the day, they'll produce at night, too.

Specific location and how muskies relate to structure can change a little at night, however, especially with fish relating to heavy weeds. Fish on hard-bottomed spots like reefs or sand and gravel may not move much after dark, except perhaps to come higher in the water column. But weed-related fish can change how they relate to spots fairly significantly at night. Rob has called it a "fountain movement," and that's an apt description. Fish seem to rise in the water column at dark, then move outward away from the weedbed itself to hold in nearby open water along its edge. The movement away from weeds can be either over nearby deeper water or to open flat areas along the weedbed's inside edge, if there is one.

Fish usually don't go far. Most often they remain within a good cast length of the weed edge. But they're easy to miss, especially when anglers have good success directly over the weed tops right at dark. Fish can seem to disappear or just shut down after full dark, and it's easy to get the impression that the night bite just isn't happening, when in reality the fish have just moved a short distance away. Why this fountain movement happens on some lakes isn't clear. It may be forage related, with muskies moving to nearby open areas to feed on suspended panfish off the deeper edge or dormant perch along inside weedlines. Legendary muskie angler and *The Next Bite—Esox Angler* columnist Dick Pearson has suggested that how fish relate to weeds after dark is related to oxygen levels in the water. The dark phase of photosynthesis consumes oxygen, perhaps lowering oxygen content in the water to the point where it becomes uncomfortable, and forces fish away from the weeds during the dark. Whatever the reason, it's an overlooked aspect of night muskie location.

Fishing in Algae Blooms

Algae blooms are a fact of life on many mesotrophic and eutrophic lakes during the dog days of late summer. Nobody likes them. It's not that muskies stop eating under these conditions. It's that finding them gets tougher when you can't see the follows and when the fish can barely see your lures. Windows of vision shrink. Opportunities for fish contact are narrowed.

Some people go home rather than fish the bloom. Others switch lakes during a heavy bloom. If there are a lot of lakes in your area to choose from, switching to a sterile, clear, oligotrophic lake is a pretty good idea. Some of us schedule our seasons this way. Save those trips to lake trout lakes for August, when your meso lakes are blue-green and opaque. This is a good strategy for another reason. Many clear, sterile lakes in the North Country are just reaching their peak in August. It's a good time to fish them. Another option is to fish larger rivers or flowages that have a strong current flow.

But what if you are "stuck" on a lake that is experiencing a heavy bloom? What if there are no alternative lakes or rivers? What if you *want* to stay on your lake because it is the best muskie lake in the state? There are strategies for you.

If you are on a large system, you will find that the bloom is not uniform. It gathers in downwind bays and the windy sides of islands. Moderate current or light wind will also stack up concentrations of algae in neck-down areas and funnels. Try fishing the upwind bays and the lee sides of islands, where you may find very clear water. You can fish midlake humps and reefs, where there is nothing to block the flow and thicken the algae. You can simply stay on the move. By covering a lot of water—as much as you reasonably can—you will increase the amount of clean water you can find and fish.

Although muskies use their lateral line and limited vision under these conditions to find forage and eat silent, naturally colored baitfish, we want to get loud. Large crankbaits that move water and also have rattles, like Jakes, and large-bladed bucktails like the Cowgirl and Shumway's Magnum Flasher widen that strike window and increase your opportunities. A muskie can sense these lures a long way off—see them, feel them. In addition to noise, flash, and vibration, use loud high-contrast colors. In blue-green algae, a black-orange lure is a good place to start.

Rock points are classic summer Canadian Shield locations. The more complex the point, with mixed rock and weeds and access to deep water, the more productive they tend to be. MARY COLSON-BURNS

One of the most exasperating aspects of fishing the bloom is that you can't see follows. End every cast with at least an L-turn, the start of a figure eight. How much of a figure eight or oval you complete before firing your next cast is a function of how well you can see into the water and—let's be brutally honest—how much faith you have in the spot. If you saw a mid-50 on that spot once before, you may want to finish every cast there with a good figure eight, at least when the visibility is essentially zero.

Countering Fishing Pressure

Muskies definitely react to and adapt to fishing pressure, and if you're going to continue to be successful during seasonal peaks of pressure, you need to react and adapt as well.

Fishing pressure can be a dilemma when it comes to both location and presentation. Enough fishing pressure can shut classic spots down under most conditions. There's no doubt that muskies will remain on classic mid- to late-summer structure even though they're pressured heavily if these spots provide what muskies need in terms of cover and food. But catching them using conventional tactics can be tough. Fishing well-known "community spots" using the same methods as other anglers will almost inevitably result in diminishing returns.

Fishing even well-flogged spots can be worth it, however, if you can find ways to fish them differently than everyone else. A key to doing so successfully is being aware of what conventional wisdom is for the body of water you're on. Knowing what other anglers are up to can give you a lot of information you can use to find alternatives. Consider this example: Lake X has always been known as a good bucktail lake. Most of the summer, most of the anglers are tossing big bucktails, because that was the hot item at the sport shows last winter. So fish on classic spots see lots of bucktails. Most lures they see are fairly high in the water column and probably moving fairly slowly (not many anglers burn big bucktails).

From that information, there are a couple options to explore. One is where lures run in the water column. Pressured fish using the edge of a weed flat or deep weedline may not rise up to lures running 3 feet down, but they may respond to a slow-rolled spinnerbait or a deep-diving crankbait.

Each option presents a different set of triggers, at a different level in the water column from what fish normally see. Speed and lure size are other potential adjustments to pressure. A small, very fast-moving bucktail may trigger a response from fish that will only follow larger, slower bucktails.

Timing is another way to beat pressure. Be aware of what time of day most anglers are on the water. If the majority of anglers aren't on the water until 8:00 a.m. and stay after dark, consider early mornings. On many of the waters we fish, community spots are productive even with conventional tactics early in the morning. There's a definite advantage to being the first person to fish a spot. On some waters, we won't fish community spots unless we're the first ones there. So get up at 3:00 a.m., fish until the other boats show up, and be gone before the pressure is on.

There are, of course, many other variables to play with when it comes to adapting to pressure. Lure size, color, speed, even boat control (which direction you work spots from) can all be opportunities to create separation between you and other anglers. What's important to remember, though, is that the objective isn't simply to be contrary. Zigging just because the other guy zags is often not enough. Throwing topwaters over 100 feet of water just because nobody's doing it likely won't gain you anything if the fish aren't there to catch. You still have to keep fundamentals—like finding fish based on time of year, forage and cover availability, and selecting the right lure for cover conditions and the type of structure—in mind in order to be successful. Adapting to pressure is a matter of finding different answers to the same puzzle than the other guys, but the puzzle pieces still have to fit together in a sensible way.

Another method of countering pressure is seeking out populations of unpressured fish in otherwise pressured waters. There's never a time when all the fish on a body of water are doing the same thing—using the same kinds of structure, feeding on the same type of baitfish, or holding in the same depth of water. Certainly the majority may be set up in a similar pattern—large weed flats, for example. But it's likely the majority of the fish also receive the majority of the pressure. Meanwhile, in other areas of the lake or on other types of spots, smaller groups of fish may be completely overlooked by most anglers. Fish get overlooked for lots of reasons. They may be holding on spots that are too difficult for most anglers to fish, like thick slop bays filled with coontail. They may be using spots that don't look like muskie spots, like bland-looking shorelines, or microversions of more classic spots, like small rock piles or small, isolated weedbeds.

Finding these types of spots takes time—and a willingness to explore off the beaten path. Our friend and *The Next Bite—Esox Angler* regular contributor Dan Craven often finds these areas by simply driving around lakes looking for them. Early spring, just after ice-out, is a great time to look for new spots. The water is usually at its clearest, and even last year's weedbeds can be spotted fairly easily.

Obviously you won't be able to fish these spots where there are closed seasons, but mark them on a map or with a GPS for when the season's open. Not all secondary spots will pan out, and only by fishing them a few times under good conditions will you be able to judge a spot's potential. Again, it's a time commitment. But the good news is that most of these types of spots are fairly small and can be fished fairly quickly. Even better news, those that do prove to hold fish can be productive year after year, and chances are, you'll have the spot to yourself.

Whatever the particulars, fish on secondary spots or nontypical structure are likely a smaller percentage of the population than muskies using classic structure. Seeking out isolated fish means making a conscious decision to fish for fewer muskies in terms of the number of fish you're casting to. But, they're also a portion of the population that sees little to no fishing pressure. Which is easier to catch? One fish out of a hundred that get pounded day after day on classic structure? Or one fish out of ten that never sees a lure?

The sports metaphor for this approach to pressure is "winning ugly." It's often more work than simply doing the obvious, or following the crowd. Thoroughly fishing a shallow weedbed so thick that no one else will fish it is more physically and mentally demanding than joining the conga line of boats that are fishing the community spots. But if you're willing to put in the work, winning ugly can be the best way to win big on pressured water. Fish in overlooked areas can definitely be easier to catch under a wider range of conditions than fish that are harried and harassed around the clock. Big fish that aren't pressured are much more likely to make a mistake. And let's be honest—catching fish on spots nobody else knows about while the rest of the herd is flailing away bumping elbows on the same old spots as always is definitely satisfying.

CHAPTER NINE

Early Fall
(Early September to turnover in the northern tier)

Early fall begins with the first sustained decline in water temperatures. The change from summer to fall isn't a dramatic one. It's a case of gradual environmental changes. Water temperatures start dropping through the 60s. As the water cools and the sun gets lower in the sky, weeds begin to die off. This triggers a time of gradual transition, as summer patterns fall apart and fish start to move to fall locations.

The most obvious cause-and-effect relationship is the loss of weed cover and how that relates to the entire food chain. As shallow minnows and baitfish lose their cover, they become easy targets for predators. This change in when and where prey is available and vulnerable changes muskie behavior as well. Muskies may begin to shift to deeper edges or move altogether to take advantage of impending baitfish migrations, or they may move extremely shallow.

There's no hard rule for muskie behavior in early fall. Changing environmental conditions can mean frequent changes in activity levels and location, and combinations of factors can change things rapidly. Sun-warmed flats in the afternoons may experience spikes in insect life, igniting the entire food chain for brief periods. Many lakes have fall frog migrations that trigger furious shallow gamefish activity. There are several reasons fish of all sizes will move up onto dead weed flats at times. Meanwhile, in other areas of the lake, the entire food chain gradually moves out to the breaklines and deep hard-bottomed spots.

Another factor that affects early-fall muskie location is fish migration. On sprawling reservoirs and flowages—which, by definition, have one or more large incoming rivers—there can be huge migrations of baitfish and gamefish. Muskies are opportunistic. If feeding opportunities are concentrated on an established migration route, the muskies will be there.

Sometimes these migrations can have a multiplier affect on the concentration of fish populations. There are baitfish (e.g., ciscoes and whitefish) that spawn in the late fall. Even though the spawning doesn't occur until much later, on the larger systems these baitfish will start to move toward their spawning areas with the first signs of early fall. On these same systems, larger gamefish sometimes migrate toward their wintering areas. When the migration routes of the fall spawners intersect the migration routes of predators, we have the multiplier effect—and a concentration of muskie food.

Although concentrations of fish will be even stronger in the late fall, things are moving in that direction. But let's first look at the early days of the transition.

Early-fall muskie location shouldn't be all that difficult. But people seem to make it so. The undeserved rap on early fall is that it's a time of poor fishing. It doesn't have to be that way. On one hand, the challenge of early-fall muskies is similar to the challenge of spring muskies. In early fall we have to determine where the muskies are in their transition from the weed flats and shallow rocks of summer to the deeper edges and hard-bottomed deep waters of late fall. But figuring out the transition is a bit easier in the fall than it is in spring. On opening day we usually have to ask questions before we hit the water. We make our best guess based on the answers to those questions. When early fall comes, we have already been fishing muskies for several months. We can see the changes coming and gradually adjust as the transition begins.

There is a way to stay on the fish all the way through the transition of early fall. First, be out there in late summer so that you know where the muskies are and so you can see the changes coming. Then be prepared to react—to make small adjustments—as the changes in weed growth and water temperatures occur. The key here is to anticipate these changes. You know they are coming, so have a game plan in place. Don't be one of those muskie anglers who are flummoxed every year when early fall arrives, weeds begin to die, and summer patterns start to fall apart.

Early fall can be a time of fantastic muskie fishing. Many of the veterans and pros catch their biggest muskies of the year in mid-September. Be one of them.

Tactics and Techniques

Before the summer patterns start to break down, before the water temperatures begin to steadily drop and the weeds die off, we should have a game plan based on fish activity over the past few weeks of the summer period. We know that fish can be at all depths, from the extreme shallows to deep hard-bottomed spots, so we need to be versatile. The single-trick pony of summer (burning in-line bucktails or throwing topwaters all day long) won't cut it.

We know in advance that as certain signs appear, we'll want to try fishing a little deeper, a little slower, and, on some waters, with lures that are a little bigger. One of those certain signs is the behavior of the muskies. When burning an in-line bucktail over shallow weedbeds doesn't produce a strike or a follow for several hours and over a range of weather and time of day variables, *that* is a sign. It's a sign that even outweighs water temperature and weed conditions. When summer tactics and presentations stop working, it's early fall. You knew it was coming. It's time to break out those early fall presentations.

Presentation

As muskies move out of the dying weedbeds to the edges and breaklines, move a little farther out from your summer spots so that you can cast to the deeper edges. This is a great time for slow-rolling big spinnerbaits along the drop-offs outside weed flats; along shoreline walls; across deep points, humps, and saddles; and into inside turns when the fishing is tough. Slow-rolling is one of the best ways to fish deep and tight to structure at the same time. And it's not hard to do.

Let your spinnerbait drop to the depth you want to fish, and then retrieve it slowly. Crank your handle just fast enough to keep the blade thumping, but not so fast that the lure rises toward the surface. The lure should come to you straight up from beneath the boat. You can let the spinnerbait drop all the way to the bottom, halfway down, or to any depth you want. Some two-angler teams will try to work two different depths—with one angler fishing a heavier, smaller bladed spinnerbait near the bottom, while the other fishes a lighter, larger bladed lure that sinks more slowly about halfway down.

For slow-rolling, single-blade spinnerbaits are best for a few reasons. First, a single blade telegraphs a lot more thump back to the angler. Hits on slow-rolled spinnerbaits can be surprisingly subtle—more of a solid *thunk* than a typical muskie smash. If the blade stutter-steps, set the hook. Feeling that change in vibration is harder with tandem blades that tend to smooth out and reduce the thump effect. When you work a spinnerbait deep and slow, that thump tells you what's going on down there. The other reason a single-blade spinnerbait is best for slow-rolling is because the lure "fishes" on the drop. All the way down, that single blade "helicopters" as it drops. The thump and the pulsing lure body attract strikes. Spinnerbaits get hit on the drop every day. Tandem blades tend to flop around and tangle themselves—not always, but often enough to be less effective than a single blade.

Along with spinnerbaits, jigs are also a primary tactic in early fall, especially on clearer bodies of water. With so many more traditional fall tactics, like jerkbaits and cast or trolled cranks, jigs don't often find a place in the arsenal for most fall muskie anglers. They should. Few baits better cover the range of location possibilities with less fuss, from fish deep on hard-bottomed edges, like points and reefs, to middepth flats where muskies prowl the remnants of summer's weedbeds, to shallow sand, rock, or gravel bars. Fewer still cover the range of potential fish moods you're likely to find in fall so thoroughly. Like spinnerbaits, jigs can be fished at virtually any depth and rival them in versatility. They can cover large areas relatively quickly when searching flats or be used to carefully poke and probe deep weedlines for fish tucked in remaining green weeds. Or do both on the same cast.

Jigs like the Bait Rigs Esox Cobra jig dressed with a rubber skirt and a thumper-tailed plastic, like a Lunker City Salt Shaker, cast like a bullet on a flipping stick or light bucktail rod. With a sharp, thin-diameter single hook and no-stretch superlines, hooking fish at long distance isn't a problem.

Retrieves with jigs aren't complicated, which is part of the beauty of it all. You can catch a lot of fish just by holding your rod tip at about the ten o'clock position and reeling steadily, pausing for a second or so every few feet to let the jig do a dive and glide briefly. It's better, though, to work the jig a little. Reel steadily, but nod the rod tip as you reel. Not a true lift/drop—you aren't bass fishing—but rather a subtle, steady nod of 4 or 5 inches performed with your wrist. Pause periodically.

Or start at ten o'clock, reel as you lift the rod tip to 11:30, then drop the rod back to 10, reeling back down as your rod tip drops. The jig will rise and fall, doing a steady stutter-step shimmy, then briefly stall and swim down before scooting off again. As you cover flats and edges, count the jig down to whatever depth necessary to run it right over the tops of any remaining weeds. If you hang up on a weed stalk, a sharp snap of the wrist will usually free it. A typical cast might mean starting your retrieve immediately when the jig lands, scooting the jig over shallow sand or an inside weedline, then pausing in the middle to allow the jig to sink a ways as you bring it into deeper water. Strikes on jigs nearly always occur as the bait drops. The feeling is a solid and satisfying *whump*. At times the line will simply go slack as a muskie overtakes the jig and rushes forward. Most fish will be hooked either solidly in the corner of the mouth or right in the roof of the mouth. Few baits are more fish-friendly.

Early fall is also a time to increase the size of your lures. If you were using smaller search baits in summer—lures that were easier to burn—then let the dropping water temperatures remind you to move up in size and

Early fall is prime time for casting jigs. Top to bottom: Musty Mayhem Stick 'Em Jig, Esox Research Co. Jig-A-Beast, Bait Rigs Esox Cobra with twister tail, Berkley Power Swim Shad on Owner jighead, Bait Rigs Esox Cobra Jig with shad trailer. DAVE OLSON

slow down your retrieve. It could be argued the season's baitfish population has grown through the summer, so a larger lure is more likely to match the forage base in size. But another reason larger lures work well is that they force you to slow down a little.

Ten-inch jerkbaits and 10-inch Believers and Jakes really come into their own as the water cools. Work the jerkbaits and Believers over reefs and flats that top out in the 4- to 8-foot range. Muskies will come up for these big, slow-moving meals passing overhead.

For getting down on the edge a bit more, work a 10-inch Jake or Triple D with whatever twitch-pause-rip-pause series of moves you can manage. The operative word is "work," but be sure to work the bait slowly. Try to make it lurch and flash in place, with minimal forward movement toward

Early-fall shield baits, clockwise from top right: Windels Magnum Harasser, Eagle Tail, Musky Mayhem Cowgirl, Shumway Flasher, Musky Mania 10-inch Jake, 10-inch Suick, Drifter Tackle 10-inch Believer, Lindy M/G Spinnerbait. DAVE OLSON

the boat. Reel just fast enough to take up slack. This presentation seems to infuriate otherwise neutral muskies. Strikes are surprisingly violent.

Throwing big bucktails and spinnerbaits is another way to slow down a little in the early fall. The larger blades and bulkier hair of M&G Spinnerbaits, Eagle Tails, and Magnum Harassers force you to slow down, and these three lures in particular have been catching trophy-class muskies for decades.

In the past few years, some of the hottest fall lakes in Minnesota have been producing mid-50-inch muskies. A significant number of these monsters have been caught on lures that take the word "magnum" to the next level. Double-bladed Cowgirls (tied with a high-flash material called Flashabou) and Shumway's Magnum Flashers (tied with marabou and a dash of Mylar) are the major culprits. Both of these lures have a pair of #10 Colorado blades. The blade size alone will remind you that these are big-fish, prime-time lures.

Another option for early fall, especially on lakes with large weed flats, is trolling jerkbaits. Once a popular technique, it's a method that seems to have been forgotten by many muskie anglers today. It's still one of the most efficient and effective methods for quickly covering middepth weed flats.

While weed die-offs are certainly a harbinger of fall, weeds don't die back at a uniform rate. Some weed species die sooner than others, and some remain green well into late fall and even under the ice. During summer, when weed growth peaks, weed flats can be solid mats of weeds that are nearly unfishable with anything but a surface lure or spinnerbait. By early fall, though, at least some weeds have died back, leaving a patchwork of pockets, lanes, and holes between remaining clumps of green weeds. Muskies that have been buried in these weeds or have been holding along flat edges move onto the flats to take advantage of the forage species like perch and panfish that are rapidly losing the cover provided by dense weeds. Covering these flats by casting works, but it's time-consuming and not the most efficient means of locating fish scattered across a large area.

Jerkbaits are an excellent trolling option in these conditions. Not only does the erratic action of a jerkbait trigger fish, the depth control offered by a floating jerkbait makes it easier to fish over weed flats, where weed growth might come to within just a couple feet of the surface in places. Trolled jerkbaits need to track straight and be able to handle speeds from 2½ to 4 miles per hour without rolling over or "blowing out." Well-tuned

CANADIAN SHIELD MESOTROPHIC LAKES AND EARLY-FALL TROLLING

For a few reasons, trolling for muskies on Canadian Shield mesotrophic lakes in summer is not as productive as casting. Although summer trolling can be very effective on oligotrophic lakes or on the flatter, comparatively featureless basin lakes more common in the northern United States, it just doesn't work very well on meso Shield lakes. The probable reason for this is that meso Shield lakes have so much available forage in the weeds and on complex weed/rock reefs and weedy island saddles. The muskies can find all the food they need up in these tight untrollable spots. They can spend most of their time in weedbeds or in their favorite nooks and crannies, foraging in ambush mode. They have no need to prowl the edges of the basin to search for food in the summer.

In early fall, that pattern starts to break down. Weedbeds collapse, baitfish move toward the edge of the basin, and some baitfish and gamefish start to gather in migration mode. You can see all this because you are making less contact with muskies on the summer spots.

It's trolling time. Not 100 percent trolling like you can have in late October, but part of the time for sure. It's time to get out the Jakes and Believers (or maybe even the jerkbaits and spinnerbaits). It's time to start mixing in a few hours of trolling every day. How many hours? The fish will tell you that.

Trolling is by far the most efficient way to find out if muskies have begun to prowl the edges of the basin looking for baitfish. Trolling is the best way to find a concentration of suspended baitfish or a migration route. You can sometimes see the baitfish on your graph. But the muskies will tell you if you have found the right spot.

(See chapter 10 for a detailed description of fall trolling techniques for Canadian Shield mesotrophic lakes.)

Suicks work, as do Sledges, but the classic trolling jerkbait is the Bobbie Bait. Bobbies track well and have a subtle shimmying swim when trolled. Plus the rounded body provides a lot of buoyancy—an important part of the system.

To troll jerkbaits, run baits between 75 and 100 feet behind the boat. For most muskie trolling techniques, parking the rod in a rod holder is standard practice, but with jerkbaits you need to work the lure as it's trolled, so hold onto the rod. Casting jerkbait rods work, but longer, somewhat softer rods in a typical bucktail action are easier to work, and the lighter power cuts down on the number of lost fish. To work the lures, simply sweep the rod forward 3 to 4 feet then follow the rod back to the starting position, keeping a nearly tight line, let the bait swim for a few feet, and

Trolling jerkbaits, top to bottom: Big Daddy, Suick, Schutt's Sledge, Bobbie Bait. DAVE OLSON

repeat. Sitting down to work baits like this with just your arm is tiring to say the least. You're better off standing and working the lures by twisting your upper body back and forth while the rod stays tucked under your arm. Worked in this manner, the lure surges forward, pauses and rises slightly, swims steadily for a few seconds, and surges forward again. Use the buoyancy of jerkbaits like Bobbies to keep from fouling your lure. Pay attention to your electronics as you pass over clumps of weeds, and slow down to float lures over thicker patches.

Shallow fall muskies are something of a puzzle to a lot of early-fall anglers. Conventional wisdom says that the onset of fall spurs an immediate migration to deeper edges for muskies. While it's truer later on in fall, on some waters early fall means a significant movement of muskies into shallow water. Sometimes it's extremely shallow water—2 or 3 feet. Muskies move across weed flats to hold along inside weedlines or move up onto sand or gravel shorelines, on top of rock or gravel bars, into beds of hard-stem bulrushes.

Inside weedlines can occur because bottom composition changes from softer bottom to shoreline sand or gravel, or because wind and wave action in shallow water prevents sustained weed growth. Whichever, inside weedlines, and often the sand or gravel flats between them and shore, are prime early-fall spots. Look for areas adjacent to summer weedy habitat, and often it's as simple as fishing the inside weedlines of the same weedbeds you've been fishing since summer peak. Generally speaking, distinct weedlines in 4 to 6 feet of water produce better than weedbeds that just gradually peter out very near shore. Edges are definitely a key. Fishing these areas isn't complicated. Cast across them or parallel to them with bucktails, run topwaters over the top of them, or slowly twitch a crankbait like a Bomber Long-A or 10-inch Jake.

Early fall is, somewhat surprisingly, one of the best times of year for topwaters. Pop-pop baits like the Musky Buster Top Walker, the Lac Seul Turbo from American Hardwoods Lures, or the Nature Vision Rumbler can call fish in from a long ways when worked over shallow, patchy weed flats, along sand or gravel shorelines, or over reefs and humps. Early in the morning, or right before dark, topwaters worked over what had, during

Sara Kimm cradles an early-fall muskie caught casting a deep weed edge. ROB KIMM

midsummer, been thick, nearly unfishable slop weed flats can produce some huge fish. Muskies cruise these now-open flats searching for perch and panfish in remaining clumps of weed growth. As water continues to cool, more subtle baits like the Topper Stopper or walk-the-dog topwaters may outproduce noisier baits, but topwaters continue to be effective right up to turnover.

Particularly on some of Minnesota's large lakes, hard-stem bulrushes attract early-fall muskies in significant numbers. The best rushes are adjacent to summer habitat like weed flats, and "clean" rush beds with sand or gravel bottoms are definitely superior to beds in softer bottomed areas with thick sandgrass or a growth of junk weeds. Within a bed of rushes, small points and fingers along the edge, thicker clumps, or lanes and pockets within the bed give fish an edge to relate to. For fishing rushes, nothing's as effective as a spinnerbait, although buzzbaits like Mike Ruff's Buzz Dog or Jack Shriver's Hi-Jacker can be a close second at times. Weedless jigs like the ERC Jig-A-Beast, Bait Rigs' Esox Cobra Magnum, or Musky Mayhem Stick 'Em Jigs dressed with large twister tails or thumper plastics are also good options—and not one fish see very often. Using treble-hooked lures of any kind is a no-go in rushes. Not only is it inefficient (fouled lures waste casts), it's also, to be frank, irresponsible because of the habitat destruction it can cause. When rushes are cut off beneath the water's surface, as often happens when you snag them with a lure, they usually won't grow back. On lakes like Leech and Cass in Minnesota, once-popular rush beds have nearly disappeared as a result of anglers tearing them up with snagged lures. It may be decades before they re-grow—if they ever do.

CHAPTER TEN

Mid- to Late Fall

(Late September to ice-up in the northern tier)

The mid- to late-fall muskie-fishing period starts with a whimper and ends with a bang. The whimper is the period known as turnover. The bang is the prime-time bonanza of big muskies on the bite. The bang tapers off at the bitter end of open water because metabolism slows as water temperatures approach freezing. But even with that slowing, the last days of open water are big muskie days.

Fishing the Turnover

There are several reasons fishing the turnover can be tough. When the lake mixes, debris and sediment on the bottom are stirred up. Water clarity can turn to mud on some systems. Algae killed off by the cold water will mat up on the surface, and it will gather in bays and necked-down channels. This can render some good spots or whole areas of the lake virtually unfishable. In addition, the mixing of oxygen means that the fish are no longer confined to water above the thermocline. They could be anywhere. Some anglers

TURNOVER BASICS

Turnover is one of the most talked about but least understood factors in fall fishing. Although turnover and its lingering effects last only a few days, turnover is a convenient excuse for poor fishing for months during the fall.

Turnover is a catchall term for several different events that occur on lakes that stratify. Water changes density as its temperature changes. The warmer the water, the less dense it is. During the summer months, a warm layer of water floats on the surface, so to speak, with water temperature gradually declining as depth increases. Eventually, when the water becomes too deep for the sun's heat to penetrate, there is a thin band where water temperatures decline rapidly. This band is the thermocline. Below the thermocline, water temperature is uniform and often low in oxygen, if not completely anoxic.

When days shorten and nights cool in fall, surface water gradually begins to cool. When surface water cools to a temperature below the temperature of the water beneath it, it sinks, displacing the water beneath it, which rises to the surface to be cooled in turn. The mixing of water as temperatures drop gradually breaks up the thermocline, returning oxygenated water to the depths. As water is displaced, it can stir up detritus and organic matter that had settled in the stagnant layer below the thermocline throughout the summer. Often lakes in the midst of turnover are cloudy, with lots of organic gunk floating in the water, and can even have a decidedly funky odor. Even on a small body of water, turnover is a significant event, and the amount of water displaced by the cooling process is massive.

Turnover is seldom a uniform event, however, and how rapidly turnover occurs can depend on local weather conditions. A slow, gradual cooldown can turn a lake over so slowly that the effect is barely noticeable. The thermocline will gradually weaken and dissolve with little fanfare. A sudden and significant temperature drop that occurs when a lake is nearly ready to turn over, especially if it's combined with heavy wind, can cause a lake to turn over literally overnight. Whether turnover is gradual or sudden can have a big effect on how much it affects fishing success. A slow, gradual breakdown of the thermocline might be barely noticeable. Sudden turnover events brought on by strong winds can mean a lot of floating gunk, cloudy water, and tough fishing.

Once turnover passes, water temperatures will be relatively uniform from top to bottom. Though day-to-day surface temperatures can fluctuate with the weather, overall water temperatures will continue a gradual, steady decline into the coldwater period.

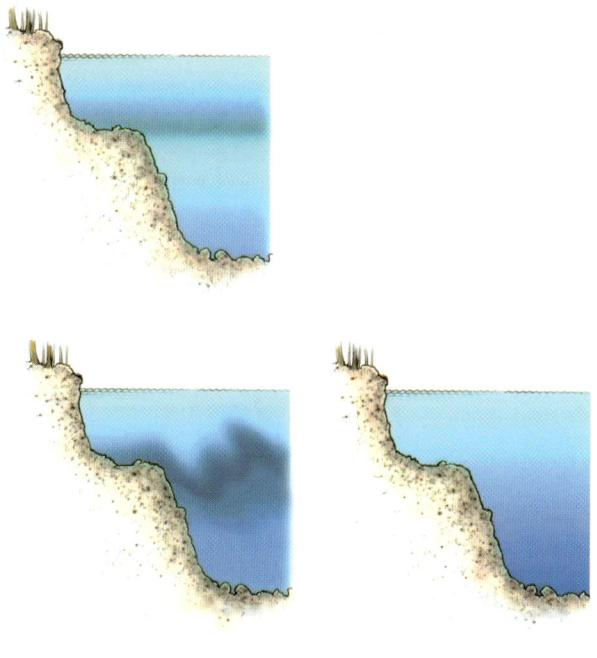

Late fall is trophy time. A happy angler, Michael Vanasse, would certainly agree. RYAN VANASSE

say that these turnover conditions turn the fish off for a week or so. Others say that the fish are still living, breathing, and eating—it's just that they are harder to find when the water conditions are bad, which seems more likely the case. Muskies need to eat.

Not all lakes or reservoir systems experience turnover. Large, shallow windswept lakes never stratify. Prevailing winds and wave action keep them mixed all season long. And reservoir systems with heavy current flow through them also escape stratification—and turnover. This is something to keep in mind if you are struggling because your lake is in turnover.

Strategies and Presentations

There are several ways to cope with turnover. The options are similar to the concept of "fight or flight." You can stay on the lake that is experiencing turnover and "fight" through it. Or you can choose "flight" and move to another lake.

The good thing about turnover is that it does not happen on all lakes— and even on lakes that have turnover, they do not all turn over at the same time. Even two lakes across the road from each other can have different timing. If one lake is 40 feet deep and 800 acres and the other lake is 90 feet deep and 4,000 acres, then their turnover dates could be ten days apart. Fish the deeper lake while the small one is in turnover, and then go fish the recovered smaller lake when the big one hits turnover. Or fish that wide shallow lake that never stratifies.

Or maybe you are fishing a huge Canadian Shield lake, like Eagle or Lac Seul in northwest Ontario. In lakes that big, there are several basins separated by narrows and channels. Even in large reservoir systems with slow current changes, some basins are dead-enders, entirely removed from any current flow. On these systems you can just switch basins. Move from basin to basin looking for sections of the lake that are not in turnover. It may only be a ten-minute boat ride from a murky section with floating muck to a clear water section where you can actually see follows and strikes.

But what if you don't have these options? What if you are on a single-basin, stratified lake 100 miles from any other muskie lake, and it is obviously in turnover? It's time to fight.

It's harder to see follows, so it's hard to stay confident. The best way to combat this is to fish proven productive spots, action spots. You can fish the most obvious community spots, because fishing pressure should not be a problem. Start shallow, but fish quickly, and move from the tops of reefs and flats to edges and out to open water 50 or even 100 yards out from the edges. With oxygen at all depths, the baitfish and the muskies can be deep or shallow. The fastest way to strain several depths is to troll with the legal limit of lines out, using lures that run shallow, medium, and deep. The water is unusually murky, so big, loud lures will attract the most attention. This is a time for loud, noisy crankbaits with rattles or spinnerbaits and bucktails with large blades for maximum vibration. Loud also means colorful lures that contrast with the water's color.

Fish the known migration routes. If you found concentrations of baitfish before the turnover, especially if you found intersections of migration routes, then continue to fish them during turnover. But mix up your depths a little. Fish up shallower near those routes, and fish deeper. If you established productive *late* fall spots the previous fall, check them out now. And be persistent. Be there when the fish turn on again. It will be well worth it.

On some bodies of water, turnover seems to push fish extremely shallow. It's almost as though they're attempting to avoid the disruption in the basin by leaving it entirely. Especially on smaller, single-basin lakes, turnover can be a time to simply put on a bucktail or a twitch bait you can fish quickly, set the trolling motor on high, and go beat the banks. Simply cover water, and hope to catch shallow fish holding on shoreline rocks, downed trees, or even docks and boat lifts. It's not sophisticated to be sure, and simply flogging shorelines isn't a technique we'd endorse very often, but it can be effective during turnover.

Fishing Fall Prime Time

Late fall, after the lake has settled down from turnover, offers arguably the best fishing of the year for large muskies. Many folks pass this idea off as hype. But for those willing to give up stalking deer, shooting ducks, or watching football on TV to brave bitter cold in a boat, late fall affords prime time muskie fishing.

Like summer, late fall is a period of relative stability for muskies once they've completed their early fall transitions and turnover has passed. Shallow weeds have mostly died—driving shallow-weed forage out to the breakline. Open-water pelagic baitfish move in to the breakline to stage for fall spawning. Baitfish and gamefish that migrate toward inflowing rivers are stacked up and concentrated on their migration routes. All of these factors combine to focus muskies on deep edges. Yes, there are afternoon movements on sunny days to shallower flats or remaining weedbeds. But most of the time, most of the food chain is stacked up on deep edges and along migration routes.

On large lakes and reservoir systems in late fall, you should look for the biggest, most obvious obstacles to travel (migration). Look for huge points, funnel areas, classic big structures. One trick: Tack your lake map on a wall. Then step back 10 or 15 feet and identify the most obvious obstacles to travel. Try to identify macrostructure, rather than microstructure. In the fall it's often the big stuff that matters.

The same principles apply on smaller bodies of water, although of course on a smaller scale. On lakes without significant large structure like points or large reefs, smaller points—often weed points that may still have green, deep-growing weeds like coontail—will attract fish that have shifted off shallow and mid-depth flats where they spent the summer. Inside turns that cut into flats, or simply sections of steep breaklines, can also concentrate fish that have either moved in from open water or vacated the shallows as weeds died off.

Strategies and Presentations

Trolling is the most efficient way to fish large lakes and reservoir systems in the fall. Most of the fish species in the food chain are relating to edges and walls and migration routes.

The advantage of trolling is that it puts your lures on the edges and walls and migration routes 25 to 50 miles per day, depending on your trolling speed and time on the water. The disadvantage is that you will only cover edges, flats, and open water. Fish that are up in the tight spots, such as inside turns, will be hard to reach. More on that later.

Trolling Mesotrophic Lakes

Trolling on large stained or dark-water mesotrophic lakes in the fall produces numbers of medium-size muskies, as well as many 4-footers. Lake of the Woods on the Minnesota-Ontario border is a typical example. But a number of U.S. lakes and reservoirs also qualify. Troll Jakes and Believers in 6 to 12 feet of water at speeds of 2½ to 4 miles per hour. Sometimes, cranking the speed up over 5 miles per hour will trigger strikes on a slow day, but this is usually not necessary.

The important thing is to cover as much good classic edge structure as possible. We have found that the midlake reefs and small islands are usually not worth the effort. Troll mainland edges and huge islands only—all the better if the edges drop into a main or at least a significantly deep basin.

It's OK to run a spread of different lures, actions, and colors. But it's much more important that your lures are making frequent bottom contact than anything else. Lures bouncing off a rocky bottom as they pass over a point or hump trigger strikes. If you're too timid to get in there and bang your lures along the edge, you will catch fewer muskies. It can be a tricky business. There are several things that can help you avoid trouble.

One serious consequence of running tight to structure for 50 miles at 4 miles per hour is that you can occasionally run aground. Trolling with a big, expensive motor and a stainless-steel prop will make you too cautious. We recommend using a small kicker tiller motor for trolling. Run the

Fall trolling baits, top to bottom: Musky Mania Ernie, Musky Mania 10-inch Jake, Drifter Tackle 8-inch Believer, Drifter Tackle 10-inch Believer, Musky Mania 14-inch Jake, Esox Research Co. Triple-D. DAVE OLSON

motor on the shallow drive setting so that it will kick up on contact. Run a cheaper and more forgiving aluminum prop on your kicker. Tiller-steer kickers will give you much more control on tight turns than a linkage to the main motor's steering wheel.

The next bad consequence of high-contact trolling—but far less serious—is snagging your lure on the bottom. This can cause break offs and cutoffs, and the loss of an expensive lure. Or, more expensively, a bad snag can cause your rod to break or even your rod holder to snap off. Even if nothing breaks, a solid snag will force you to reel up and circle back to recover the snagged lure. There are ways to prevent all this.

Use a very light drag setting. If your drag slips a little when you accelerate suddenly, you have it about right. Don't worry about not hooking fish. The forward momentum of the boat will set hooks, even with a light drag. And the light drag will stop things from breaking if you do hang up. Use an 8-foot or longer trolling rod that is soft and forgiving—almost a slow fiberglass action, and slightly heavier power than a downrigger rod. Many anglers use Dipsey Diver rods for muskie trolling. Soft rods seem to bend back easily with any bottom contact, allowing the lure to bounce out of the would-be snag.

Use strong no-stretch line like Cortland Master Braid or Spectron to offset the soft rod and light drag. Use a 3- to 6-foot stranded steel cable leader in the 130- to 170-pound-test range to prevent cutoffs on rocks. High-quality line-counter reels like the Shimano Tekota help you run your lures at precise and repeatable distances. This lets you know where your lures are running relative to the depth you are trolling. For example, you can run your inside (closest to shore) line at 40 feet back, your middle line at 50 feet, and your outside line at 60 feet back. These are typical settings for running 10-inch Jakes in 8 feet of water on a sharp-tapered edge.

It's 6:00 a.m., 19 degrees. Boat's full of snow. What are we waiting for? ROB KIMM

If you employ these techniques and tricks, you will avoid most of the pitfalls and hazards. If you focus on edges and migration routes and keep your trolling lures in the water, you will experience your best muskie fishing of the year.

Trolling Oligotrophic Lakes

Trolling on oligotrophic (trout water) lakes in the fall is a low-numbers proposition. But the chances of contacting a true monster are about as good as you can get. Whitefish Bay on Lake of the Woods and Eagle Lake, both in northwest Ontario, are typical examples. But a number of U.S. lakes also fit this description, as do the northeast shore of Georgian Bay in Lake Huron and the Thousand Islands area of the St. Lawrence River as it flows into Lake Ontario.

Lakes we refer to as "trout water" may or may not actually have lake trout in them. But they fish the same. The important similar factors are water at least 70 feet deep (but usually deeper) and an abundance of open-water pelagic baitfish that move in to rock/rubble shorelines to spawn in the fall. Other common characteristics include very clear water, a relatively sterile weedless environment, and a lot of great-looking rock structure.

The biggest challenge when all the shorelines and islands and reefs look textbook perfect is to find the ones that hold fish. When muskies are rare—few and far between—your search is for signs of a food chain rather than for the needle-in-a-haystack trout water muskie. The best way to search is by trolling. You should focus your efforts on two types of structure—cisco spawning areas and migration routes.

Troll the perimeters of main lake basins. Look for classic rock/rubble shorelines adjacent to the main basin. Look for schools of baitfish on your graph. Plowing through clouds of baitfish does not necessarily guarantee that you will contact muskies, but it will put you close. Mark the schools of baitfish, and then troll nearby points, walls, humps, and saddles. Then troll the open water just outside the baitfish. Muskies will not be *in* the schools. They will be nearby, looking for stragglers.

Troll the major points and corners in the lake. The biggest obstacles to fish migration will see the most traffic. High-traffic areas attract opportunistic feeders, especially the fearless ones at the top of the food chain.

The good news is that trolling on trout water lakes is a lot simpler than trolling on dark meso lakes. Occasional bottom contact is still a good thing. It still triggers strikes. But instead of banging along in less than 10 feet of water, and sometimes banging your prop into rocks, you can troll in 20 to 100-plus feet of water and relax a bit.

The main difference here is not the fish. Muskies are muskies. The difference is water clarity and light penetration. Increased light penetration puts the muskie's ambush zone down at 20 feet or more instead of at 5 or 10 feet, as it is on many meso lakes. This means you can move out to deeper water and troll deeper running lures. The upside of the water clarity difference is that muskies can see your lure a long way away. A lure running 30 feet out from a shoreline wall can be easily seen by a muskie cruising the wall. A lure running 20 feet deep can be easily seen by a muskie cruising at 35 feet. Maybe that sounds like a stretch, but think about it. It's less than the length of your boat—for a 50-incher, two flicks of the tail and it's on your bait. The point is that running your lures extremely close to structure is not all that important. Constant contact isn't as necessary to draw a fish's attention. So there is less need to run a low horsepower kicker motor and an aluminum prop. It doesn't hurt, but it's not a requirement.

Troll with Ernies, Cisco Kids, Believers, Triple Ds, and other deep-running crankbaits in 20 feet of water or deeper, usually in the range of 2½ to 4 miles per hour. Experiment with higher speeds, even up to 8 or 9 miles per hour when conditions are tough. Make a pass hugging the walls and steep edges, and then move out to deeper water. Stay on the move. Look for schools of baitfish on your locator. Look for rock/rubble shorelines near the main basin. Find the migration routes.

On trout waters you are looking for signs of life, for any niche in the food chain. The water is sterile, so any one element of the food chain, even lake trout, is a good thing. The rest of the food chain won't be far away.

Trolling Stateside Waters

Trolling on stateside muskie waters is somewhat different from trolling on either mesotrophic or oligotrophic Canadian waters. Although there are exceptions (Minnesota's Lake Vermilion being one example), most stateside muskie waters don't have continuous rock shorelines, and in many cases muskies are more concentrated on key pieces of structure rather than spread out on small shoreline points and pockets. Open-water trolling

Ciscoes are key forage species on many muskie lakes throughout the year, especially in fall as they migrate toward their spawning areas. ROB KIMM

can also be effective on these types of waters when pelagic forage fish like ciscoes are present.

Although the type of structure may differ, the basic principles remain unchanged: Basin edges and baitfish movements are key pieces of the puzzle.

On lakes with ciscoes, edges next to basin areas that provide summer cisco habitat are usually the place to start. As with shield lakes, large main lake points, inside turns, and steep shoreline edges along main lake basins are key areas. Large main lake reefs or humps can also hold late-fall muskies, although unless there are very prominent pieces of structure on a particular body of water, midlake humps or reefs don't seem as consistently productive as shoreline-connected structure.

Unlike shield lakes, however, weedlines are often part of the picture on these mesotrophic waters, and can be a challenge when trolling basin edges and breaks. Run too shallow, and your lures are fouled with weeds. Obviously, good boat control and paying close attention to your electronics are important. Lure selection can help you troll tight weed edges better, too. Deep-diving baits like 10-inch Believers, ERC's Triple-Ds, or Musky Mania Ernies can be run at depths ranging from 12 to 16 feet on relatively short lines compared to medium divers like Jakes, which helps on tight turns as you follow an edge.

Trolling weed points and inside turns effectively, especially when your ability to maneuver is somewhat restricted by a weedline on one side, can require repeated passes to cover an area thoroughly. A plotting GPS unit is a huge help in keeping track of what you've covered on a particular piece of structure and what you haven't.

As you troll, watch your electronics for remaining clumps of green standing weeds. Deep weed growth on inside turns and on the leeward sides of points can often remain green long after weeds on shallow flats have died off. A large clump of green cabbage along a main lake point can be a fish magnet in late fall. Fish cruising the break will position in these remaining weeds, and a single green clump of weeds can produce multiple fish throughout the entire fall period.

Pay attention to the depth of the weedline and how it relates to the break into deeper water. Points and flats with slower tapers may have bare stretches between the weedline and the break itself. For example, weed growth may end in 14 feet of water, while the first break into deep water occurs in 17 feet, leaving a barren shelf between the weed edge and the break. Like clumps of green weeds, these shelves can be key locations throughout the fall. They're worth multiple passes, especially when the shelf juts out into the main basin of the lake.

While many fall basin edges have weeds, they aren't necessary to hold fall fish. Gravel, sand or rock points, or bare sand breaklines can also attract muskies when they're adjacent to basin areas. Trolling these areas without weeds to contend with is obviously easier. It's usually simply a matter of selecting lures that run roughly the depth of the break into deep water. On large lakes, large midlake rock reefs produce a lot of big muskies in the fall. Trolling these areas is similar to trolling rocky shield lakes—contact with structure is a key trigger.

On clear lakes, trolling passes off the edge of the reef but within 200 yards or so of it can also be effective. On some lakes, midlake rock reefs can literally swarm with staging ciscoes. It seems logical to simply troll right on top of the reefs where the food is. But in reality, trolling off the edges

Late-fall conditions can be brutal, but the fish are worth braving the cold. JACK BURNS

seems to be more productive. It seems counterintuitive, but it's definitely been our experience on several waters. It makes sense in a way when you consider the predator-prey relationship at work. Ciscoes aren't likely to appreciate large predators like muskies parked right on the reef.

True open-water trolling is also an option on some of these lakes. Who knows why, but some lakes are just plain better than others for open-water trolling in the fall. And they can be better to the point where it's clearly the best option for catching fish consistently. The only way to see if this is the case is to try it.

Fall tactics for open-water muskies don't differ much from those used during early summer. Crankbaits like Jakes, Ernies, Believers, and Stalkers, either flatlined behind the boat or behind boards, can be trolled over basin areas where you've located concentrations of baitfish or seen large arcs on your electronics. Big baits like 14-inch Jakes and 13-inch Believers can excel on some waters. What does differ in late fall, though, is that muskies after turnover seem to use a wider range of depths, depending on how deep schools of baitfish are holding. You may need to run lures at a wider variety of depths, from near the surface to 25 feet, and experiment until you identify a key depth range to focus on that day.

Fall Casting

Trolling puts your lures on the edges and walls and migration routes 25 to 50 miles per day. But with trolling you can only cover edges, flats, and open water. Fish that are up in the bays with stringy dead weeds or tucked into tight ambush spots, such as inside turns, are hard to reach. Casting allows you to reach those areas and thoroughly fish them. Even if most of the big muskies caught in the late fall are caught trolling, who wants to write off the rest? Do you? We didn't think so.

On Canadian meso lakes, especially on warm sunny late afternoons, west-facing dead-weed bays come to life. Even though the weeds are nothing but lifeless bent-over strands, schools of crappies or perch may move up into the warmer water. Muskies, frequently in frenzied wolf packs—often 30- to 45-inchers—will move into the same bay and tear into the panfish. Or sometimes a solitary 50-incher will cruise into the bay, looking for a weak and vulnerable easy meal. Show her a slow-wobbling

Believer or a gently twitched Suick. Mix in some long pauses. Hang on.

Some muskies are not out there cruising the edges and moving into bays when they sense baitfish. Some may have nice little ambush spots that continue to give them everything they need. Maybe it's a deep notch in a boulder reef or a tight inside turn on the edge of one of those classic migration route points. Maybe it's a warm south-facing rock wall in the back of a huge, sloppy, weedy 5-mile-deep bay. None of these fish can be caught trolling.

Probably the best way to get into these tight spots is with a single-spin spinnerbait. Cast the lure tight to structure, into the notch, up against the wall. Let the lure drop with the single blade helicoptering down. When the lure makes contact with the bottom, point the rod at the lure and slowly retrieve (slow-roll) the lure back to the boat. Mix up straight retrieves and slow rod-pumping retrieves. Fish the spinnerbait like a jig-spin rig. This technique seems to be incredibly discriminatory. Small fish often ignore this presentation—maybe it isn't frenetic enough—but big fish climb all over it.

On U.S. waters, casting remains an effective approach as long as it's not too miserable physically to do so. The edges of weed flats that may still have patches of deep-growing green weeds, isolated green clumps on the top of the flat, points, and inside turns should all be cast to. Finding clumps of green weeds by trolling edges then fishing them thoroughly by casting to them is an extremely effective combination approach in late fall.

Lure selection can depend on depth and cover, but single-spin spinnerbaits are definitely a good option, for all the reasons described above. Slow-moving jerkbaits like weighted Suicks or Reef Hawgs worked slowly along breaks and over remaining green weeds are a classic late-fall tactic. Crankbaits like Ernies, Jakes, and Triple-Ds worked like a jerkbait with twitches and pauses through deep weed edges or along the edges of rock or gravel points also can be effective. Large soft plastics excel in cold water, and Bull Dawgs or giant Red October tubes rigged on 2- to 3-ounce jigheads have become extremely popular with late-fall anglers over the past few years and have the definite advantage of being able to work at virtually any depth.

For efficiently covering large weed flats with scattered clumps of green weeds, single-spin spinnerbaits are a good choice, as are twitched crankbaits like Jakes. Jigs like the Bait Rigs Esox Cobra can be cast long distances and worked at a variety of depths, depending on depth and cover conditions, which makes them a versatile choice. They're not big baits, but a Bomber Long-A can be a very good fall bait for covering large flats. They can be worked very erratically, and the flash and near walk-the-dog action can really call fish in from a distance. Plus they cast like a bullet for covering large areas. They're perhaps one of the most overlooked options for fall casting.

Although much of the fall activity is focused on basin edges, there are situations where muskies will move extremely shallow in the fall, sometimes as shallow as 2 or 3 feet of water. On at least some lakes these shallow fish are relating to ciscoes that are moving into these areas, apparently at night. On calm days it's not unusual to see chewed-up ciscoes lying on the bottom, yet we rarely see ciscoes during the day. We do, however, see muskies, plus suckers and other baitfish that are apparently feeding on cisco eggs. Obviously, trolling isn't an option for reaching these fish. On other lakes, bare sand shorelines, shallow rock points or rock piles, or the tops of sand or gravel bars attract fish, ciscoes or not.

Finding these shallow areas isn't easy. It takes time and effort. Especially when it comes to sand shorelines or gravel bars, it's much like rock walls on oligotrophic shield lakes. A 20-yard section out of a 300-yard long stretch will hold all the fish, with no discernible reason. The good news is that when you *do* find areas that hold fish, those areas seem to attract them year after year.

Although it definitely flies in the face of tradition, topwaters can be one of the most effective ways to catch these shallow fall muskies. We've caught muskies on topwaters in water as cold as 38 degrees. Subtle topwaters definitely seem to work better, especially on clear lakes. Walk-the-dog baits like a Doc or a J-Walker from American Hardwoods are a first choice; subtle propbaits like a Topper Stopper can also be good. Unlike other times of year, topwaters don't seem to be very effective in waves in cold water. Calm, overcast conditions are better, and midday— from 10:00 a.m. to 3:00 p.m.—seems to be the best time of day for topwaters. In windier conditions, or early and late in the day, minnow baits like a Jake or Bomber Long-A, high-riding jerkbaits like unweighted Suicks, single-spin spinnerbaits, or a ½-ounce Bait Rigs Esox Cobra jig scooted over the sand are good options for shallow fish. Muskies in clear, cold, shallow water can be extremely spooky, so long casts and a stealthy approach is a must.

Yes, fall casting can be cold on the fingers. When the air temperature is well below freezing and your hands are wet, it can be brutal. But to catch the fish that are not reachable by trolling, you're going to want to give it a shot whenever you can.

Fishing Very Late—Pre Ice-up

As water temperatures continue to decline, muskies on some bodies of water shift off the shallower breaks to deeper, secondary breaklines or steep edges plunging into deep water. For most muskie anglers, these are fish that have fallen off the radar. They're either too deep for traditional trolling or casting tactics when holding on secondary basin breaklines, or they're difficult to spot on electronics on steep, nearly vertical drops along the basin edge. On bodies of water with a lot of steep breaklines, where depths go from 12 or 14 to 35 or 40 feet in a boat length, fish on steep edges can be the predominate pattern throughout the fall period. Yet because they're tough to target with traditional approaches, these lakes have reputations as tough lakes in fall, where fishing success is sporadic, and the fish, for whatever reason, just "won't bite."

Whether it's in extreme late fall, or on reputedly tough lakes with lots of sharp breaks, vertical jigging is by far the most efficient and consistently effective means of catching muskies, but it's a technique very few anglers even attempt and even fewer give serious effort.

Vertical jigging for muskies certainly isn't a traditional approach outside a few isolated geographic areas. But vertical jigging for fall muskies works for the same reasons vertical jigging works for other species in cold water, whether it's walleyes in the North or winter reservoir bass down South. When fish are holding tight to steep breaks, and boat control and, more

Overlooked by most anglers, jigging in late fall can be extraordinarily effective for coldwater muskies. Top to bottom: Shumway Fuzzy Duzzit, Red October Giant Tube, Bait Rigs Esox Cobra Jig, Musky Innovations Bull Dawg. DAVE OLSON

MUSKIES AND DEEPWATER RELEASE

One of the most troubling aspects of fishing for muskies in deep water late in the fall is that fish can sometimes have difficulty adjusting their swim bladder when they ascend too rapidly from deep water. It's not a matter to take lightly. Fishing deepwater muskies, as effective as it is, does carry some risk for the fish. A muskie's swim bladder is below its center of gravity, so when muskies are bloated with air and can't adjust their buoyancy, they simply roll over on their backs. Especially when fish are hooked near the bottom in deep water, it's critical that they be brought to the surface slowly, allowing them to adjust their buoyancy somewhat during the fight. It's not unusual to see bubbles coming to the surface as a fish is fighting—an indication that the fish is releasing air from its swim bladder. How deep is deep? Generally speaking, any time fish are hooked deeper than 25 feet, it's time to take it easy

on them coming up. We all want to get them to the boat, but Fuzzy Duzzits are outstanding hookers, and few fish get off, even when brought up slowly. Another advantage of bringing fish to the surface carefully is that when you do so, fish seldom roll in the line, as they're prone to doing in cold water. Heavy upward pressure seems to make them spin for some reason.

Though most fish stay deep when allowed to do so, especially in frigid water, occasionally a hooked fish will rocket to the surface immediately. There's little you can do, and if they're coming from deep water, they may have trouble with their buoyancy. Unhook the fish as quickly as possible, then help the fish stay upright in the water by holding it gently by the tail with another hand supporting the belly (waterproof gloves really help). A cradle or large net can be a big help. Given time, and if they get some help staying upright, most fish can

important, lure and lure depth control are required to get a lure into a fish's strike zone, nothing is more precise than a vertically presented lure.

Having quality electronics and knowing how to tune and interpret your depthfinder is more important for vertical jigging than with any other muskie tactic—even open-water trolling. Fish holding on steep breaks or tight to bottom in deep water can be difficult to spot on electronics, but large-screen color units like the Lowrance LCX-112C or LCX-37C make spotting fish a lot easier. You can make a case for color units being a dispensable luxury with other muskie tactics, but there's no doubt they help catch fish with vertical jigging.

For most vertical jigging, there's little need to go beyond one lure: the Fuzzy Duzzit. This large, banana-shaped blade bait was invented by Hayward, Wisconsin, guide and tackle manufacturer Bill "Fuzzy" Shumway several years ago and is simply the best tool available for vertical jigging eventually adjust their swim bladder on their own. Occasional small bubbles from the gill openings or mouth are a good sign. Fortunately, cold water is very forgiving with releasing fish. (We don't recommend fishing for muskies in deep water during summer. Fortunately, there's seldom a need to during most of the season.) Some have recommended gently stroking a fish's belly from the ventral fin toward the fish's head to help release trapped air, but it's an open question as to how much it helps. One thing to absolutely *not* do is attempt to "fizz" fish by sticking them with a hypodermic needle. Getting the precise location for inserting the needle is something not even an experienced fish physiologist will attempt with confidence, and if you're a few millimeters off, piercing vital organs is a near certainty. Just don't do it. If you support the fish and allow it to adjust its buoyancy gradually, it will eventually swim off on its own.

Releasing muskies caught in deep water can be problematic if fish are brought to the surface too quickly. Be patient, bring fish up slowly, and let fish caught from deep water recover before releasing them. SARA KIMM

muskies. Large tubes on jigheads, or even large soft plastics like Bull Dawgs can work, but none have the combination of flash and vibration, plus a fluttering fall, that the Fuzzy Duzzit has. What's more, the Duzzit's knife profile cuts the water exceptionally well moving forward, allowing you to keep your line vertical or nearly vertical below the boat, even when moving forward at a surprisingly brisk pace for a vertical presentation.

Fishing the Fuzzy is painfully simple. Drop the lure to the bottom, reel up enough to lift the bait 10 inches to a foot off the bottom, then steadily lift and drop. Lifts don't need to be particularly high—2 to 3 feet is enough—nor especially sharp. It's a steady but strong lift more than a rip. Pause briefly between each lift, but only for a second or two. It's vital to follow the lure down with the rod tip on each drop so that the lure falls on a semitight line. Most hits occur as the lure falls, and they can be easy to miss, even when you're watching carefully. We're used to muskies

Color sonar units like those from Lowrance are extremely helpful when searching steep breaks for baitfish and muskies holding tight to the bottom. DAVE OLSON

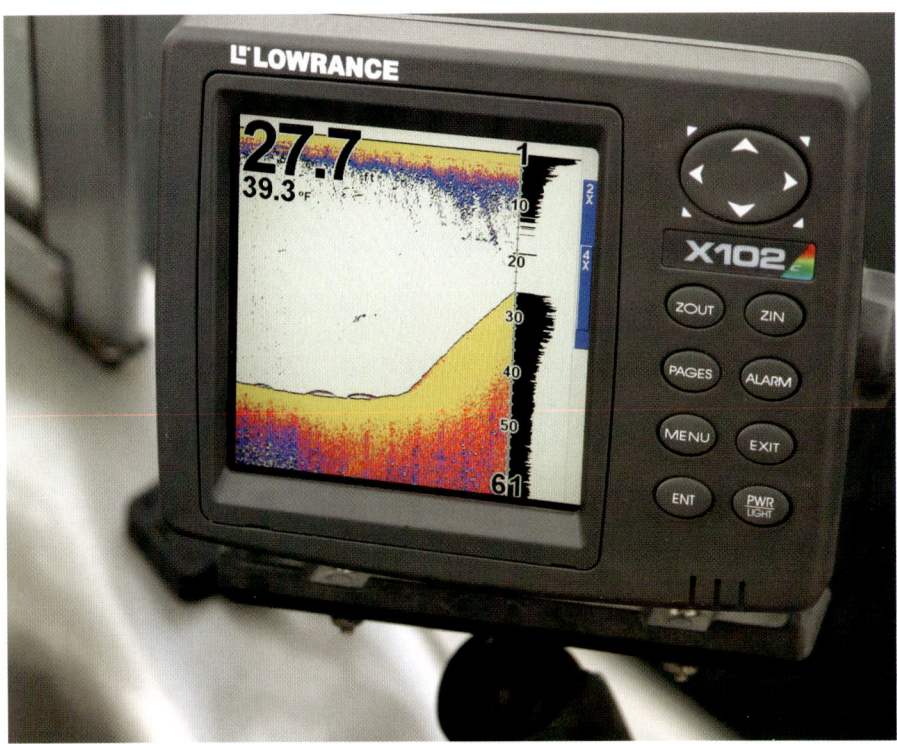

smashing lures, but most hits on a Fuzzy Duzzit are surprisingly subtle. Often there's just sudden weight when you begin your next lift. The fish is just there. If you feel dead weight, or the line suddenly goes slack, set the hook hard. Occasionally muskies will hit as you lift the rod and nearly take the rod out of your hands, but it's the exception rather than the rule.

Key spots for vertical jigging are steep breaks along main lake basin edges. If these breaks have small points or large inside turns along them, so much the better. Steep inside turns between good summer locations like weed flats or points can be positively magic in late fall. Secondary breaklines can also be very productive. A secondary breakline is simply an additional, deeper drop-off into the lake's basin. A typical example may be a large flat that breaks from 15 into 25 feet of water, with a deep shelf or gradually sloping flat that extends for a distance toward the main lake basin, then breaks quickly from 28 to 45 feet or more of water. The 28-foot break is a secondary break that definitely can hold fall muskies, especially near ice-up. Yet few muskie anglers even consider looking for them there.

Even with a Fuzzy Duzzit, you can't cover water at much more than a walking pace, so choose your areas carefully. Finding life in the form of schools of baitfish and hopefully larger marks that indicate muskies is key, and it's not unusual to search several potential areas with your electronics before wetting a line. Like many kinds of muskie spots, though, certain spots prove themselves over time and can be worth fishing even if you don't spot baitfish or muskies. But proven spots aside, if you don't mark life you're often better off moving on. It's truly a case where your electronics, not your lures, are the search tools.

When you've found a break with potential, cover the breakline from top to bottom, using your trolling motor to move up and down the break. Keep track of the bottom with your lure as you move up and down the break by occasionally dipping your rod tip to allow the lure to touch bottom. Let out more line or reel in as necessary, but keep as close to bottom as possible most of the time. Watch your graph, and you can usually see your lure on the screen as you jig. You'll also see muskies come up to hit it.

As you reach the base of the break, it's often worthwhile to venture slightly out into the basin to search bottom transition areas where hard sand, gravel, or marl turns to mud. Deep bottom transitions attract walleyes, perch, suckers, and other muskie forage in late fall and can be quickly searched with a combination of your electronics and lure.

CHAPTER ELEVEN

Bringing It All Together

There have been several themes to our discussion of muskie-fishing tactics. Bringing these themes together into a cohesive tactical approach can put you into that elite group of muskie anglers who catch most of the muskies. And keep in mind—these themes were not developed in a research lab or ivory tower. Nor were they based on the experiences of one or two hard-fishing authors. These themes, these tactical suggestions, are based on working with and fishing with highly successful muskie anglers all across the muskie range—from northwest Ontario to West Virginia, from the St. Lawrence River to Colorado.

Let's review the themes and look at ways to bring them together.

Muskies as Apex Predators

A theme that is spelled out early and underlies every chapter of this book is the fact that as an apex predator, muskies in any naturally reproducing system represent a very low population density. Yes, some small heavily stocked lakes are loaded with several muskies per acre. But these situations are rare and unnatural. For 99.9 percent of the waters we fish, simply finding a muskie is our focus. We are not looking to make contact with vast schools of muskies, but with one muskie—or at least with one muskie at a time.

Muskie anglers at every level above novice are more concerned with understanding, tracking, and finding muskies than they are with nuances of presentation.

Knowledge of Muskies' Seasonal Needs

Our breakdown of tactics into seasons of the fishing year is based on the simple fact that a muskie's choice of habitat, its location, its depth in the water column, its attitude, its aggressiveness, its feeding frequency, and even its relative boat shyness are all influenced by the muskie's basic biological needs. As the seasons move from the spawning period through the summer peak and into late fall, we need to adjust the focus of our search.

Knowledge of Muskies' Environment

In addition to understanding the muskie's basic seasonal influences, we also must be students of the muskie's local environment. We look at everything from lake classification, to water clarity, to current, to structure like weeds, rocks, and stumps, and to the other fish species and how their behavior affects muskie behavior. We even look at the influence of fishing pressure—the behavior of other muskie anglers—and adjust our tactics accordingly.

If we continually adjust to the seasonal and environmental changes, we will have a good chance to stay "on fish." That's most of the battle right there.

Lures and Equipment as Tools

We devoted our biggest chapter to lures and tackle. But we did not do that because we think there are secret lures or presentation tricks to reveal, or to hide. Lures and tackle really are just tools. The first job of these particular tools is to hook and hold a muskie so that you can land it and safely release it. The fish are very big, and they fight hard. They have razor-sharp teeth. The tackle must stand up to a lot of wear and tear.

The next job of the tools known as fishing lures is to be cast or trolled in front of a muskie and trigger it into striking. Our analysis of lures that we recommend for various seasonal or environmental situations is based on how they meet the needs of that situation. Do they run deep or shallow? Are they weedless and snagless when you fish in heavy cover? Do they cast well into the wind? How fast can you fish them? How slow? How do they behave on a pause?

Selecting the right tool for the task at hand means asking a lot of questions about the situation at hand. But the question we *don't* ask is:

Muskie fishing isn't always about the fish . . . MARY COLSON-BURNS

What do the muskies want? What they want is a cisco, a perch, a sucker.... We don't fish with those. We may have lures that look something like them, but that's probably more for our sake than the fish's. What matters when it comes to presentation is finding a tool with a set of capabilities that fits the situation.

Safety and Safe Catch-and-Release

Along with the tools used to fish for and catch muskies, we also acknowledge the importance of other tools, such as fish-friendly oversized coated nets that allow you to keep a netted muskie in the water while you work on removing or (preferably) cutting hooks so you can release her. Long needle-nose pliers, a powerful hook-cutting tool, and a sturdy jaw spreader are essential tools for extracting hooks. The two most important reasons to keep that fish in the water:

1. **It lets the water support the weight of the muskie.** Lifting a large muskie out of the water puts stress on the fish's internal organs. Keeping the fish floating in water means that its organs are supported naturally.
2. **It lets you keep the muskie's head under water as much as possible while you remove hooks, so the fish can breathe.** Whenever the fish's head is out of the water, hold your own breath so that you know how frequently to get it back into the water.

We also discussed factors that can lead to unsuccessful release and the need for an awareness of the cumulative effect of stress-causing conditions like high water temperatures or heavy wind and waves.

As your skill at catching muskies grows and you catch more fish, the obligation to practice good catch-and-release techniques grows as well. The more fish you come in contact with, the greater potential effect—positive or negative—you have on the future of the fishery.

The Role of Goals and Styles

When we describe goals, we aren't talking about good goals versus bad goals—valid versus not valid. A tournament angler has a goal of catching a few decent-size muskies. A guide with novice clients or a few young children does not have the luxury of fishing for a solitary monster. The novices or youngsters would grow impatient. This guide has a goal of action. The more muskie strikes in the shortest amount of time, the better. A muskie-fishing veteran, fishing solo, has plenty of time and no pressure to produce action. His goal is most likely a 4-footer—or bigger.

And we can see that goals vary from day to day. On the first day of a weeklong trip, your goal may be to survey the lake and locate fish. On the last day, you are pounding those three monsters you saw that week.

The point regarding goals is that they influence your fishing style. If your goal is action and contact with several fish or just taking a quick survey of the lake, then your style will be to fish fast and high in the water. You will cover a wide swath of the lake but not worry about fishing various depths or tight nooks and crannies. But if your goal is to catch one monster on your last day of a trip, then your style will be to slow way down and thoroughly fish a few great spots from top to bottom, inside and out.

The Role of Fishing Philosophies

We looked at two philosophies, which we can call "hunker down and learn" and "explore and chase." Again, we do not claim that one philosophy is bad and one good. Explore and chase is the approach the led to the "discoveries" of Wabagoon, Lac Seul, and Georgian Bay. It also led to the incredible fishing pressure we are seeing on the hottest lakes in Minnesota and Wisconsin. This is fishing pressure that naturally follows publicity about mid-50-inch muskies. Explore and chase is a philosophy that has often led to spectacular catches.

The hunker down and learn philosophy is a way to drop out of the chase but still have a great chance to catch very big muskies. This approach has you hunker down on one big lake or an area of lakes and take the time to learn them as thoroughly as possible. This approach allows you to stay on the fish throughout a range of seasons and conditions. You can stay with them as they move through their seasonal transitions, and you can continually monitor changes in the muskies' environment, not just water and weed conditions but also other fish species and other anglers—all factors that influence muskie behavior. Hunker down and learn is a philosophy that often leads to spectacular catches that you never hear about.

The Role of Fishing Pressure

We looked at the fact that although it's an apex predator, the muskie actually does have one predator above it—the muskie angler. More so than probably any other freshwater gamefish, muskies adjust their behavior, their location, even their feeding times in response to fishing pressure. They also can get conditioned to the popular/standard/acceptable presentations that they see day in and day out. They may move away from a constantly fished spot. They may drop deeper than the constantly fished depth. They may even get bored with certain popular fishing methods. A muskie may be provoked into striking something it has not seen before, but when it sees the same lure 1,000 times in a month, it may not react to it at all. We refer to very popular ways to fish a given lake, the most popular spots and times of day as the "conventional wisdom" for that water.

It's good to learn the conventional wisdom for the waters you plan to fish. Learn it—and then run in the opposite direction. We use an old football expression: "running to daylight." Apply that thinking to a few aspects of the local conventional wisdom at a time. If everyone fishes shallow, try fishing deep once in a while. If everyone retrieves lures fast, fish slow. If everyone goes left, go right once in a while. Mix it up. Stay true to some of the conventional while you experiment with other factors. If you want better results than everyone else, you have to fish differently from everyone else. Have fun with it.

Time on the Water

Everyone talks about "time on the water," but few understand what the phrase really means. We often hear the phrase spoken in jealousy: "That

guy has so much time on the water, no wonder he catches so many muskies," or "If I could spend that much time on the water…"

OK, we can't all spend every day on the water. But that's not the right way to look at it.

Try using the phrase like this: "What can I do to best use *my* time on the water?"

It seems as though a lot of people approach learning how to fish muskies as a search for the silver bullet, the true secret to muskie fishing success. They may even think those who *do* consistently catch big muskies are holding back that secret but that if they listen carefully enough, someday the secret will slip out. But the answer is not a certain lure or a secret presentation nuance that is passed along by members of a cult. The answer is not in your tackle box. The answer is not in anyone's tackle box.

You already have everything you need. You have done your homework. Your tackle is ready to go. Hooks are sharp, leaders and line are strong, rods and reels are balanced to your lures. You understand the seasonal and environmental factors. You know how to search for muskies. You know how to thoroughly fish the big-fish spots. You have picked a lure that is the right tool for the conditions. Now, just fish.

The question is: "What can I do to maximize my time on the water?" The answer is to fish hard. Don't stare into your tackle box, pondering what to try next. Don't waste time with that stuff—there are no answers in there. The answer is in the water. Just fish.

The secret to muskie fishing success—the only secret—is this: Keep your lure wet.

Opposite: Catch a nice one and let it go. Let them all go. JERRY SONDAG

INDEX

ABOUT THE AUTHORS

Jack Burns is editor emeritus of *The Next Bite—Esox Angler* magazine. Jack has fished muskies for more than thirty years throughout Wisconsin, Minnesota, and northwest Ontario and has published muskie-fishing articles in *In-Fisherman* and *Peterson's Fishing* magazines. Jack was the muskie columnist for *Minnesota Outdoor News* from 1990 to 2004 and has been a guest speaker at Muskies Inc. chapter meetings throughout the Midwest.

Rob Kimm is senior editor of *The Next Bite—Esox Angler* magazine. A former instructor at *In-Fisherman*'s Camp Fish, Rob now pursues muskie and pike in Ontario and Minnesota. He is a frequent contributor to *In-Fisherman* magazine and is the featured muskie columnist for the *Minnesota Outdoor News*. Rob holds a master of fine arts in creative writing.